SEATTLE UNIVERSITY SKILLS DEVELOPMENT SERIES

Criminal Procedure

JOHN B. MITCHELL
Professor of Law
Seattle University Law School

RICK T. BARRON
Attorney at Law
Santa Barbara County Public Defenders

THE MICHIE COMPANY
Law Publishers
CHARLOTTESVILLE, VIRGINIA

COPYRIGHT © 1995

BY

THE MICHIE COMPANY

———

Library of Congress Catalog Card No. 95-75341

ISBN 1-55834-219-2

———

Printed in the United States of America

PREFACE

The books in the Seattle University Skills Development Series are intended to provide students with a *link* between traditional substantive courses and the world of lawyering. To accomplish this, the books in the Series focus upon how practicing attorneys think about and use a different area of substantive doctrine in their practice.

The centerpiece of each of the books is the CASEFILE or TRANSACTIONAL HISTORY. These files and histories are made up of an extensive collection of realistic documents which contain the facts the student will use to guide their representation. Here the facts of the case are not prepackaged. Rather, like practicing attorneys, the students must recognize, extract, and characterize information relevant for their representation as they sift through the documents.

Assignments, correlated to specific substantive issues in the area, then place students in a wide range of settings and lawyering tasks. Each demands that the students act as problem-solvers. All require meshing an appreciation of the particular substantive law with a variety of lawyering skills as they actually put the student in the role of an attorney who is carrying out the ongoing representation of a particular client, a role in which tactics, judgment, and ethics are always at play. Each assignment also contains a series of Planning Questions which force students to think through relevant aspects of the representational situation, and Exercises in which they actually perform some lawyering tasks (e.g., draft, argue, interview, examine, counsel, present, negotiate, and such). The student is encouraged to use the extra spaces provided beneath the questions in this book to make notes, quickly answer questions, or provide a full written response on request.

Criminal Procedure brings to life the world of criminal attorneys, both prosecution and defense, as they work within the framework of this significant body of doctrine. Criminal Procedure doctrine in fact circumscribes the Criminal Justice System in a number of interrelated ways. Sometimes, it provides rules for the administration of criminal trials, such as discovery and joinder or severance. Other times, it determines whether there will be a trial at all, such as when principles of speedy trial and double jeopardy are brought to bear. Often, however, it acts as constitutionally-inscribed rules of evidence in which the Fourth, Fifth, and Sixth Amendments are used to define what governmentally obtained evidence will or will not be excluded from trial.

This text follows a case from investigation and evidence gathering to arrest and, ultimately, the commencement of a conspiracy trial. Along this journey, the students must engage in strategic planning and problem-solving, as well as resolve a series of ethical dilemmas, as they prepare for a range of hands-on performances. Here they will conduct an interview with a police officer, argue to trial and appellate courts about the legality of automobile searches and photo identifications, put on direct-examinations and conduct cross-examinations at a hearing to suppress evidence obtained in a *Terry* stop or in a police interrogation, draft search warrants, etc. Throughout, they will work with a realistic casefile that includes transcripts of a suppression hearing and a police interrogation, an Information, numerous police reports, evidence, lab reports, a search warrant and supporting affidavit, evidence logs, and other relevant materials.

EDITOR'S NOTE

In this case study, the following conventions have been used regarding the time and place of events:

- All events take place in the jurisdiction of Cascadia.
- The current year is designated as Y-0, the year before as Y-1, etc.

TABLE OF CONTENTS

INTRODUCTION
The Conspiracy Prosecution

Introduction.

On July 30, Y-0, Nettletown prosecutors filed an Information charging Thomas Katsinski, Gilbert Jardine, William Bean, Rachel Klein, Edward Broil, Kevin Lumus, and Ralph Freely with conspiracy to copy, reproduce, and distribute copyrighted material without authorization (so-called "bootlegging" or "piracy"). James Dailey was listed as an unindicted co-conspirator. Thomas Katsinski, Gilbert Jardine, William Bean, and Boyd Stern were charged in the same Information with knowing possession of unauthorized duplicated copyrighted material (Appendix A). In a separate Information, filed March 5, Y-0, Miller Frone was charged with knowing possession of unauthorized duplicated copyrighted material and possession of marijuana (Appendix B).

What follows is the history of a police investigation that begins with an encounter at the airport and, through a series of stops, warrants, searches, arrests, interrogations, and show-ups, leads to the filing of the Informations. These materials also cover pretrial issues of jeopardy, joinder and severance, discovery, and speedy trial.

CHAPTER I
The Case Begins

I.1. An Encounter at the Airport

Throughout these materials you will be alternatively taking on the roles of defense attorneys and prosecutors. Since most search and seizure issues which arise in court begin with the conduct of some police officer(s) in the field, however, you must develop some sense of how these issues looked to the *police* at their inception. Accordingly, for this initial assignment, you will imagine that you are Airport Security Guard S. Rosten. As you will see, you will have a number of difficult decisions to make as events unfold.

Review Appendix B in CASEFILE and pages which your instructor will assign in your Coursebook.

<u>EXERCISES</u>.

Assume the role of Security Guard Rosten. Be prepared to explain your decisions at *each* of the following nine "decision-points." At each decision-point, consider: 1) What legal issues do you face? 2) What legal and practical risks do you take by your action or inaction? 3) What legal and practical options do you have available at this particular decision-point?

1) Decision-point #1 —

Rosten, you are working the day shift at the Nettletown airport ... You've just gotten some stale cheese crackers sandwiched around a dry layer of peanut butter from a vending machine when your walkie-talkie begins to crackle —

Airport [AP]: Rosten, are you there? Over.
R: This is Rosten. I'm in the ticketing area of Eastwinds Airlines
        near the Skylift Lounge. Over.
AP: Rosten, this is Nettletown Police Officer Smith. Be on the
        lookout for an adult white male, medium height, 5'9", about
        170 pounds, brown overcoat carrying blue garment bag with
        a red stripe. He was dropped off about ten minutes ago at
        Eastwinds' departures by a man believed to be intoxicated on
        narcotics. Stop, identify, and question the suspect as he may
        be involved in drug traffic. Do you copy? Over.
R: I copy. Over and out.

You survey the ticketing area. No one fitting the description is in view. After checking the Eastwinds' departure schedule, you head towards gate 11 where the next scheduled departure is to Los Angeles at 4:15 p.m. While standing in the boarding area, you see a man in his mid-thirties coming out of the men's room. The man is closer to 5'11" than 5'9", and his garment bag has two thin red stripes, but otherwise he fits the description. As he advances toward you on his way to the boarding area, you have to make a decision —

7

CHAPTER I. THE CASE BEGINS

a)   Can you initiate the contact with the suspect passenger?*

b)   If so, what can you do?

c)   What can you say? (E.g., can you order him to halt? Ask questions about his possible involvement in drug smuggling?)

d)   What should you inform the passenger? Why?

---

*Use the spaces provided to make notes so that you can quickly answer your supervisor's questions or provide a full written response on request.

8

2) Decision-point #2 —

You've decided to approach the man ...

R: Sir, may I speak with you a moment?

Passenger [P]: (Says nothing, but stops next to you.)

R: May I see some identification?

P: (Pulls out wallet, extracts driver's license and hands it to you.) What is this about? Who are you?

R: Airport Security, sir. This will just take a minute. (Into the walkie-talkie) This is Rosten at Eastwinds departure lounge calling Nettletown Police Officer Smith; do you copy? I have an adult white male here whose identification says he's Miller Frone. What do you want me to do now? Over.

a)   Have you done the correct thing thus far? Explain ...

b)   Explain why it was all right to ask Frone for his identification ...

c)   What, if any, legal effect did asking for his identification have on your encounter?

d)   Should you have immediately started questioning him about the man who you think dropped him off in order to make your actions legal?

3) Decision-point #3 —

[45 seconds later ...] No response over the walkie-talkie ...

a)   Can you continue to try to delay Frone? How long can you legally justify detaining him under current caselaw?

b)   What will you do now?

c)   What will you tell Frone?

4) Decision-point #4 —

You decide to keep Frone busy while awaiting a reply from the Nettletown Police ... It wouldn't hurt to double-check his identification against his ticket, you think ... and that whole process will take up a little more time —

R: Mr. Frone, may I see your ticket? Where are you going?
Frone: I'm going to L.A. Will you please tell me what this is about?
        (Hands ticket to you.)
R: Just routine, sir. (You look at the ticket and see that it's for coach fare on Eastwinds Flight 703 issued to M. Frone, departure time 4:15 p.m. to Los Angeles. You then hand the license and ticket back to passenger.)

a)   Did you have the right to ask for the ticket? Why or why not?

b)   Has handing back the license and ticket carried legal consequences?

5) Decision-point #5 —

[3 minutes later ...] You still haven't gotten a call back on the walkie-talkie ...

a)   Can you continue to delay Frone?

b)   It's starting to get uncomfortable standing in the middle of the airport ... probably beginning to become a bit embarrassing for Frone, too — might be better to wait in the security office. Also, the "change of scene" will take a little more time ...

        1. What legal problems are involved in taking Frone to the security room?

        2. Is there a way around these problems?

6) Decision-point #6 —

[30 seconds later ...] You decide to ask Frone to accompany you to the security room ... As long as he's there, you figure you might as well also do a warrant check on the computer — it will take more time and, who knows, it may turn up something ...

R: Mr. Frone, will you please accompany me to the security office?

Frone: I have a plane to catch in less than 20 minutes.

R: Oh, that will be no problem, the room is right over there by the women's restroom (gesturing). It will only take a couple of minutes to run a routine computer check on your license. Will you follow me, please?

Frone: Well, I guess so.

a) What are the legal consequences of your actions under *Terry v. Ohio*?*

b) Is the fact that the distance to the security room is a short one significant for Fourth Amendment purposes?

7) Decision-point #7 —

[1 minute later ...] When you and passenger Frone get to the security office, some fifty feet from the Eastwinds boarding area, you punch Frone's license number into the computer. While you are waiting ...

Frone: [objecting]: Look, I'm going to miss my flight. Am I under arrest, or what?

R: No, Mr. Frone, you're not under arrest, but I wish you would wait just a bit longer; the computer should give you a clean bill any second now, ... you won't miss your plane — if you don't have any outstanding warrants, that is.

Frone: I don't have any warrants. I've never been arrested before.

R: Well, then, you shouldn't mind waiting a few more minutes ... should you?

Frone: All right, but ...

R: But what? Have you got something to hide, Mr. Frone?

Frone: No.

---

*Issues concerning PRIVATE CITIZEN SEARCHES and Mr. Frone's possible CONSENT to Rosten's actions will be considered later in these materials.

a) What is your legal justification (other than "consent") for continuing to delay Frone?

b) What right do you have to hold him while you run a computer check? Explain ...

8) Decision-point #8 —

[5 minutes later ...] Nothing has shown up on the computer ... Having Frone behind you in the small security room while you sit at the computer and wait for a response on the walkie-talkie is making you uncomfortable—you'd like to pat-search him ...

a) What right do you now have to frisk Mr. Frone?

9) Decision-point #9 —

You decide to frisk the suspect ... At the same time, you hear a voice boom over the loudspeaker, "Flight 703 will begin boarding in three minutes ..."

14

R: Just one last thing, Mr. Frone. You won't mind if I pat you
        down for weapons, will you?
Frone: Officer, you've checked my ticket and run my license through
        the computer already. Isn't that enough?
R: Is there something you don't want me to find, Mr. Frone?
        That is your real name — Frone — isn't it?
Frone: I've nothing to hide.

You proceed to pat Frone ... In his right inside suit pocket you feel a flat solid
object, about 2″ x 4″...

a)   On what basis can you remove this object?

You reach in and pull out a box-like object wrapped in paper. Unwrapping it,
it turns out to be a cassette tape with a hand-drawn map wrapped around it. Not
feeling any of this significant, and wanting Mr. Frone to catch his plane, you start
to hand back the tape and map. As you do, three hand-rolled cigarettes fall from
the paper. One is half-smoked; and as you retrieve and inspect the cigarettes, you
realize from your training and experience that they contain marijuana. You
immediately place Frone in custody, seizing the cigarettes, tape, and map. You
then call Nettletown Police who arrive a few minutes later, arrest Frone, and take
him and the evidence away.

I.2. A Motion to Suppress

Miller Frone has been charged with possession of marijuana and knowing possession of a
bootleg cassette tape. Since the crucial evidence was obtained as the result of the search by
Airport Security Guard S. Rosten, defense counsel is bringing a motion to suppress this
evidence on the grounds that Rosten's conduct was not justified under prevailing legal
standards.

In this assignment, you will work through the suppression motion from both the
prosecution and defense sides. [Issues of CONSENT and PRIVATE CITIZEN SEARCHES will be
dealt with in other portions of these materials. *Do not* deal with either in this assignment
unless your instructor tells you otherwise.]

Review Appendices B, C, D, F, G, J, and K in CASEFILE and pages which your
instructor will assign in your Coursebook.

PLANNING QUESTIONS.

1. The nine "decision-points" in I.1, *supra*, roughly provide the basic areas of Rosten's action that will be the focus for the upcoming suppression motion. *Prosecutor*, for each area:

   a)   What facts (good or bad) are most important (i.e., pivotal)? Why?

   b)   How will you legally justify Rosten's action?

   c)   Which case(s) help you? How will you use the case(s) to support your position?

2. What do you anticipate will be the defense's argument in each area? What will be your response?

3. *Prosecutor*, as you're interviewing Rosten in preparation for the suppression motion, he says, "What are the problem areas of my testimony?" How will you respond? He then says, "Look, you're the lawyer, you know the law. I'm curious. When I took the tape out of Frone's pocket, what sort of reasons would make that kind of thing legal?" What do you respond now?

4. Does any of this make any difference? Even if the tape and marijuana get excluded at a suppression motion, can't Rosten just testify at trial to what he saw without showing the jury the actual physical evidence?

EXERCISES.
Your instructor will divide you into prosecutor or defense.

1.   *Prosecutors and Defense Attorneys*. Using the transcript of the suppression motion hearing (Appendix K) as your factual record, prepare to argue your position to the Court.

CHAPTER II
The Investigation Continues

II.1. The Searches of the Cars

The conspiracy case began to form as the result of a series of three automobile searches. While the initial search of the Camaro incident to Boyd Stern's arrest for DWI only yielded a single tape, the subsequent inventory search of that same vehicle produced a bonanza for the police — particularly rental records, charge card slips, and a parking receipt that led to the Cougar. The warrantless search of the Cougar on the police's belief that it would contain evidence of drug trafficking revealed boxes of bootleg tapes.

The defense will want to try to develop a credible theory for a motion to suppress the fruits of these searches. The prosecution will resist such efforts. In this assignment, you will work through the strategic positions of the defense and prosecution as they prepare for this confrontation. [Issues concerning STANDING and TAINT will be dealt with later in these materials.]

Review Appendices A, C, E, L, M, and N in the CASEFILE and pages which your instructor will assign in your Coursebook.

PLANNING QUESTIONS.
1. List all the evidence found as result of these three automobile searches.

2. As to each piece of evidence, what is its importance to the prosecution for 1) proving the existence of a conspiracy and 2) tying particular defendants to the conspiracy? [Alternatively: What effect will suppression of such piece of evidence have on the prosecution's presentation to the jury?]

3. Assuming the evidence is found admissible under both constitutional standards and the rules of evidence, how will the prosecution discuss it in Closing Argument to the jury?

4. For each of the three automobile searches:

   a) What legal theory will the prosecution put forth to justify the search?

   b) What will be the defense theory opposing the prosecution?

   c) What are the pivotal facts (good and bad) for each side's theory?

   Prosecution:

   Defense:

d) What are the main case(s) for each side? How will they use the case(s)?

EXERCISES.

Your instructor will divide you into prosecution or defense.

1. *Prosecutors*. Imagine you are preparing for an upcoming evidentiary hearing on defense's motion to suppress the fruits of the three automobile searches. You will put on evidence to justify these three warrantless searches. For each search, prepare an outline showing: A) each witness you will call; B) the points you will bring out in the witness's direct examination. [Be prepared to explain why you have chosen to bring out each point.]

2. *Defense Attorneys*. Make an outline of the points you would bring out on the cross-examination of each prosecution witness. [Be prepared to explain the reasoning behind your choices.]

3. *Prosecution and Defense*. Be prepared to argue over the legality of one of the searches. [Your instructor will tell you which search and the factual record on which you may rely in making your argument.]

(Note that as you develop your direct or cross-examination, you must think about how to elicit facts helpful to your theory and damaging to your opponent's. Also, anticipate how your opponent will bring out facts damaging to your case and be prepared to deal with facts both damaging and favorable in your argument.)

II.2. The Investigation Expands

With the discovery of the boxes of bootleg tapes in the Cougar, the investigation was turned over to the Tape Fraud Task Force (TFTF). That unit began an aggressive, three-step investigation. First, they wired a post office box where they believed money and information regarding the tapes were being transmitted. Then, using helicopters and satellites, they conducted aerial surveillance of the general area they thought those involved with the tapes might be located. Finally, finding a likely location through the surveillance, the TFTF sent an undercover agent, posing as a meterman, onto the suspect property.

In this assignment, you will consider the prosecution and defense perspectives on the issue whether (any or all of) these actions constitute ''searches.''

Review Appendices A, O, Q, and R in CASEFILE and pages which your instructor will assign in your Coursebook.

PLANNING QUESTIONS.

1. These three activities turned up a number of pieces of potential evidence for the prosecution's conspiracy charge. Some, however, are more crucial to the prosecution's case than others. Roughly rank the importance of these various pieces of evidence, being prepared to explain your ranking. [Alternatively: What will be the consequences to the prosecution conspiracy case if each piece is suppressed?]

2. What is the theoretical significance of whether these activities are labeled "searches" or not? What will be the legal consequences of whether or not these activities are considered searches for whether the information obtained by the TFTF is admissible?

3. As the prosecution and defense take their positions over whether or not *each* activity is a search:

   a) What are the pivotal facts (good or bad) for each side? Why?

b) What are the key cases (good or bad)? Why?

c) How will each side deal with the "bad" facts or cases?

4. *Prosecutors*. You personally believe the use of the satellites was improper, but have a plausible argument that it did not constitute a search. (In fact, you think you'll probably win in front of the judge.) What are your ethical obligations?

5. *Defense Attorneys*. All the defendants want you to represent them. Can you? How? Should you? Explain.

EXERCISES.
Your instructor will divide you into prosecution or defense.

1. *Prosecutors*. In anticipation of an upcoming suppression motion, you will interview the undercover officer who posed as the meterman. In preparing, focus on finding information regarding the issue of whether the entry was a search.

2. *Defense Attorneys*. Brainstorm how you will establish that each of these activities was a search. Be certain to anticipate both the likely response of the prosecution and any concerns that the Court may have.

CHAPTER III
The Search of "The Rancho"

III.1. Planning to Obtain the Warrant

The Tape Fraud Task Force (TFTF) has reviewed all the information obtained from: the arrests of Miller Frone and Boyd Stern; the searches of the Camaro and Cougar; a confidential informant; wiring the mailbox; the aerial surveillance; and the meterman. The TFTF now thinks they have enough information to seek a warrant to search ''The Rancho,'' and come to the prosecution for assistance.

In this assignment, you will assume the role of prosecutor in seeking a search warrant. [Issues of TAINT will be considered later.]

Review Appendices A–R in CASEFILE and pages which your instructor will assign in your Coursebook.

PLANNING QUESTIONS.

1. List all the information you now have that could support a request for a search warrant.

2. What will you argue (i.e., present in an affidavit to the magistrate) to establish that this information is sufficient to constitute "probable cause"?

3. Can you take out any piece(s) of information and still have probable cause? Which? Why might you want to do this analysis?

4. What is the minimum information from all you have that you can put forth and still have probable cause?

5. Does the informant present any problems for you? If so, how will you deal with such problems?

6. *Prosecutors*. Though you cannot articulate why, you have a feeling that the "confidential informant" is a fabrication of the TFTF. What do you do?

EXERCISES.

1. *Prosecutors*. Discuss if you think you're ready to seek a warrant. If not, what more would be helpful, and how would you suggest the TFTF obtain such information?

2. Brainstorm the (specific) scope of the warrant you will seek.

III.2. Attacking the Face of the Warrant

The prosecution has obtained and the police executed a search warrant on "The Rancho." The defense is now reviewing the warrant itself for possible grounds for attack.

In this assignment, you will consider the defense and prosecution positions as to an attack to the face of the warrant.

Review Appendices U, V, and W in CASEFILE and pages which your instructor will assign in your Coursebook.

PLANNING QUESTIONS.

1. Look at the information obtained in the search. Which is most harmful to each defendant? Why?

2. Good practitioners often create checklists. Create one for attacking and defending search warrants:

   a) List all the facets of a search warrant, accompanying documentation, or execution of the warrant that in theory might be subject to attack ...

   b) Now list the legal standard the *prosecutor* must fulfill in order to resist each of these areas of attack ...

31

3. What issues can the defense plausibly raise in an attack "on the face" of the warrant?

<u>EXERCISES</u>.
Your instructor will divide you into prosecution or defense.

1. *Prosecution and Defense.* The defense is attacking the warrant (Appendix U) on its face. Each side be prepared to argue your position to the Court.

2. *Prosecutors.* Draft a new warrant so that it is impervious to facial attack.

III.3. Execution of the Warrant

During the search of "The Rancho," police located a cabin (occupied by Ralph Freely) on the land. They entered without knocking or announcing their presence, and searched the cabin. This search is now the subject of a suppression motion.

In this assignment you will work through the adversary positions of the prosecution and defense regarding the failure of the police to give "knock-notice" prior to entering the cabin.

Review Appendices X and Y in CASEFILE and pages which your instructor will assign in your Coursebook.

<u>PLANNING QUESTIONS</u>.
1. What is the law regarding so-called "knock-notice"?

2. What is the policy behind this law?

3. Assuming the trial court rules that the police were required to give knock-notice before entering the cabin, what will be the effect on the prosecution's case regarding: a) evidence that will be suppressed; b) the consequences of losing this evidence both as to the conspiracy charge and the ability to tie each defendant to the conspiracy?

4. Focusing on the issue of knock-notice:

   a) What will the prosecution argue? What will the defense argue?

   b) How will each side answer the other?

   c) What are the pivotal facts (good or bad) that each side will seek to elicit from Officer Snopt on the witness stand?

5. *Defense Attorneys.* Assume that you go back to the scene (i.e., the cabin) to investigate. What will you look for? Why?

6. *Defense Attorneys.* Ralph Freely comes into your office and places a video cassette on your desk, saying, "The police missed this somehow in the search. Good thing. We took it while we were stoned and we're all talking and walking through the whole operation. Everything. It's all on tape." What do you do?

<u>EXERCISES</u>.
Your instructor will divide you into prosecution or defense.

1. Each side plan your strategy for the evidentiary hearing on the issue of knock-notice.

   a) *Prosecutors.* Choose your witnesses and outline the points you will bring out in each witness's exam. [Be prepared to explain why you have chosen to bring out each such point.]
   b) *Defense Attorneys.* Outline the points you will bring out in the cross-examination of each prosecution witness. Will you call any witness(es) of your own? If so, outline the points you would bring out in such witness(es)'s direct examination. [Be prepared to explain your decision regarding whether or not to call any of your own witnesses.]

2. *Prosecutors and Defense Attorneys.* Argue the issue of knock-notice to the Court. (Your instructor will tell you the factual record on which you may base your argument.)

CHAPTER IV
Tom Katsinski's Arrest

IV.1. Arresting "T.C."

Evidence located during the search of "The Rancho" and subsequent investigation potentially identified Thomas Katsinski as a prominent figure in the conspiracy. Determining Mr. Katsinski's address, police went to that location and arrested him in the mobile home he was occupying. At the time of the arrest, police did not have an arrest warrant.

In this assignment, you will explore the lack of an arrest warrant from both the defense and prosecution sides. [Issues of TAINT will be dealt with later.]

Review Appendices A, DD, and EE in CASEFILE and pages which your instructor will assign in your Coursebook.

PLANNING QUESTIONS.

1. Assume the prosecution is permitted to use all the information obtained as a result of Katsinski's arrest at trial. How will the prosecution use this information in Closing Argument?

2. If the trial court holds that the police needed an arrest warrant, what effect will this have on the prosecution's case against Katsinski?

3. Before considering the facts of this particular case, outline the general body of law concerning arrest warrants.

4. What are the pivotal facts (good or bad) for each side concerning the need for an arrest warrant in this case? Why do you consider the facts pivotal?

5. What will each side argue?

6. What problem(s) does (do) the prosecution face in its position? How will it deal with such problem(s)?

7. What problem(s) does (do) the defense face in its position? How will it deal with such problem(s)?

EXERCISES.
1. Make a list of the points that you would expect each side would want to bring out at an evidentiary hearing.

2. Your instructor will divide you into prosecution or defense.

   Prosecutors and Defense Attorneys. Prepare to argue to the Court your side's position regarding the need for an arrest warrant.

IV.2. New Information Concerning a Third Person's Home

In the course of investigation by members of the prosecutor's investigative staff, it was discovered that the trailer in which Katsinski was arrested was on the property of, and owned by, Katsinski's next-door neighbor. Katsinski was being allowed to stay in the trailer for a few weeks while he was remodeling his own home. At the time of the arrest, the police were not aware of this and had assumed that the trailer was Katsinski's and that it was located at his address.

In this assignment, you will assess the significance of this new information (if any) from the perspectives of the dcfcnsc and prosecution.

Review Appendices FF and GG in CASEFILE and pages which your instructor will assign in your Coursebook.

PLANNING QUESTIONS.
1. Putting aside the legality of the arrest for the moment, what effect (if any) does this new information have on the merits of the prosecution's case at trial against Katsinski?

2. Focusing on the arrest of Katsinski:

   a) What significance will the defense attribute to this new information? Why?

b) What will be the prosecution's response?

3. *Prosecutors*. Do you need to tell the defense about the interview with Ms. Bracken?

EXERCISES.
Your instructor will divide you into prosecution or defense.

1. Assume the trial court finds that the police should reasonably have realized that the mobile home was a third party's home, and accordingly needed a search warrant to enter. You are now before the Court of Appeals on an interlocutory writ brought by the prosecution. The appellate court wants you to address two issues:

a) What is the proper standard of review for an appellate court reviewing a trial judge's decision on a suppression motion?

b) Applying that standard to the present case, did the trial court err when it found that the officers reasonably should have known that the mobile home was a third person's home? *Prosecutors and Defense Attorneys*. Prepare to argue your positions.

CHAPTER V
The Evidence Keeps Rolling In

V.1. James Dailey's Uncle

The TFTF received information from an undercover officer at the local high school that James Dailey, who is a juvenile, was selling bootleg tapes. Police went to the address the school had listed for Dailey to interview him. The home turned out to be that of Dailey's uncle, with whom Dailey had been temporarily staying since the recent death of Dailey's father. After explaining the situation to the uncle, police were taken to the room where James had been staying. In the corner of the room was a locked trunk that belonged to James. At this point, James entered the room. The uncle told the boy to open the trunk. James refused. Finally, the uncle demanded the keys, and while the police watched, the uncle opened the trunk. Inside were a large number of bootleg tapes.

In this assignment you will analyze the significance of the uncle's cooperation from the prosecution and defense perspectives. [The issue of PRIVATE PARTY SEARCHES will be dealt with in other portions of these materials.]

Review Appendix AA in CASEFILE and pages which your instructor will assign in your Coursebook.

PLANNING QUESTIONS.

1. What are the various legal theories that justify third-party consent?

2. Explain how the facts in this case support one or more of these theories.

3. What is the significance for each side that: (a) it was the uncle's home; (b) James is a juvenile?

4. What are the weaknesses in each side's position?

5. How will each side deal with these weaknesses?

6. *Defense Attorneys*. You go to interview James Dailey. Imagine that James does not have an attorney. What are your obligations? What would you respond if he says, "Maybe I should call the prosecutor before I talk with you"?

EXERCISES.
Your instructor will divide you into prosecution or defense.

1. Prepare for a motion to suppress the tapes found in the trunk.

  a) *Prosecutors*. Outline: (1) list the witness(es) you will call at an evidentiary hearing; (2) draft the questions you will ask each witness on direct to bring out the salient points; (3) prepare cross-examination questions for any witness(es) you anticipate the defense will call.

b) *Defense Attorneys.* Outline: (1) draft the questions you will ask each prosecution witness on cross-examination; (2) draft the questions you will ask on direct of any witness you decide to call. [Be prepared to discuss the reasoning behind your questions and your decision whether or not to call any witness(es).]

2. *Prosecutors and Defense Attorneys.* Be prepared to argue the motion to the Court. (Your instructor will designate the factual record on which to base your arguments.)

V.2. Bill Bean and Another Look at Miller Frone

Bill Bean was stopped in his vehicle during a roadblock of the Big Tree area. At the request of the off-duty officer who stopped him, Bean agreed to open the trunk of his vehicle. The trunk contained bootleg tapes.

As to our old friend Miller Frone, the prosecution claims that he consented to much of his interaction with Airport Security Guard Rosten.

In this assignment, you will explore the consent issue in both Bean's and Frone's cases from the point of view of the two adversaries. [Issues of TAINT from the DRAGNET and PRIVATE PARTY SEARCHES are dealt with in other portions of these materials.]

Review Appendices C, J, K, and Z in CASEFILE and pages which your instructor will assign in your Coursebook.

PLANNING QUESTIONS.
1. How (specifically) will the prosecution use the evidence found in these two incidents? If it is suppressed, what effect will that have on the prosecution's (a) conspiracy charge; (b) cases against Frone and Bean?

2. Make a "consent checklist."

a) List all the ways you can think to legally invalidate a consent search ... [e.g., if Bean had only consented to the search of the passenger compartment, the search of the trunk would be "beyond the scope" of the consent.]

b) Which (if any) apply to either the search of Bean's automobile or Frone's person?

3. Imagine suppression motions in both Bean's and Frone's cases which focus on the consent issue. As to *each* of these motions:

a) What are the pivotal facts (good or bad) for the prosecution? For the defense? Why?

b) What will be the prosecution argument justifying the consent?

c) What will be the defense argument attacking the consent?

46

4. *Defense Attorneys*. In the Bean case, imagine that your client's story directly contradicts that of the officer so that it is his word against that of a police officer. Do you have any *general* strategic approaches to dealing with such a credibility situation (i.e., criminal defendant v. police officer) before the court?

5. *Prosecutors*. Something in your gut tells you that Fellows is lying about Bean's consent. What will you do?

EXERCISES.

Your instructor will divide you into prosecution or defense.

1. *Prosecutors and Defense Attorneys*. It is time for you to put on an actual evidentiary hearing. You will focus on the consent issue in Bean's case.

   a) *Prosecutors*. Prepare Officer Fellows, put him/her on the stand, and conduct his/her direct examination. Be certain to anticipate likely cross-examination in your preparation.
   b) *Defense Attorneys*. Cross-examine Officer Fellows.
   c) *Prosecutors and Defense Attorneys*. Argue your positions to the Court using the evidence presented at the live hearing for your factual record.

2. *Prosecutors and Defense Attorneys*. Using the transcript of Miller Frone's suppression hearing (Appendix K) for your factual record, be prepared to argue about the applicability of consent to Frone's situation.

CHAPTER VI
James Dailey Talks, "T.C." Blabs

VI.1. Analyzing James Dailey's Confession

After James Dailey was arrested, he was taken to the police station, then juvenile detention, and finally juvenile court for a detention hearing. While refusing to talk to police for most of this period of time, James eventually provided a tape-recorded confession in which he implicated himself, Gilbert Jardine, Edward Broil, and "Tom Cat."

In this assignment, you will take the role of prosecutor, analyzing any problems you may have with James's confession.

Review Appendices BB and CC in CASEFILE and pages which your instructor will assign in your Coursebook.

PLANNING QUESTIONS.
1. Time to make another set of checklists.

    a) List the various grounds (e.g., *Miranda*) upon which a confession may be suppressed.

    b) Might any of these grounds raise problems for the prosecution in this case? Explain.

    c) List all the ways the defense could attack a confession under *Miranda*.

d) Do any of the attacks seem possible in this case?

e) List all the ways the prosecution can argue that *Miranda* does not apply, even though a confession has been obtained.

f) Do any of these ways to obviate *Miranda* seem possible in this case?

2. How will the prosecution use James Dailey's confession at trial? How significant is this confession to (a) the prosecution's conspiracy charge; (b) tying particular defendants to the conspiracy?

3. Assuming the confession passes constitutional muster, under the Rules of Evidence, can the prosecutor simply play the tape to the jury in its case in chief?

EXERCISES.

1. *Prosecutors*. Work through all the problems you face in getting James's confession admitted, and how you propose to deal with such problems.

VI.2. A Motion to Suppress the Confession

The defense is moving to suppress James Dailey's confession. The parties have stipulated that the motion will be based upon the transcript of Dailey's tape-recorded statement (Appendix CC).

In this assignment, you will work through the adversary positions for the suppression motion. [Issues of STANDING are dealt with in other portions of these materials.]

Review Appendix CC in CASEFILE and pages which your instructor will assign in your Coursebook.

PLANNING QUESTIONS.

1. What constitutional grounds will the defense likely raise to attack the confession?

2. For *each* such legal grounds:

a) What case(s) will the defense use? How?

b) What case(s) will the prosecution use? How?

c) What are the pivotal facts (good or bad) for the defense?

d) What are the pivotal facts (good or bad) for the prosecution?

e) What are the weaknesses in the defense position? In the prosecution position?

f) How will the defense and prosecution deal with their respective weaknesses?

3. *Prosecutors*. Imagine you believe that James Dailey has run away. You are now discussing a plea bargain with Katsinski's attorney. Must you tell her about James's flight?

<u>EXERCISES</u>.
Your instructor will divide you into prosecution or defense.

1. *Prosecutors and Defense Attorneys*. Using the transcript of James Dailey's taped confession, be prepared to argue your respective positions to the trial court.

VI.3. Tom Katsinski Blabs to an Informant

Phil Reese was in jail with Thomas Katsinski before Katsinski bailed out. Reese now claims that, after being released, he went to Katsinski's apartment, had a little guy to guy talk, and that Katsinski confessed all. Prior to going to Katsinski's apartment, Reese had meet with members of the TFTF seeking help with his own criminal case in return for getting them some big fish in the bootleg tape racket.

In this assignment, you will assess the significance of these events from the perspective of the defense.

Review Appendix HH in CASEFILE and pages which your instructor will assign in your Coursebook.

<u>PLANNING QUESTIONS</u>.
1. What is the importance of this evidence for the prosecution's case against Katsinski?

2. Assuming the information is found to be admissible for trial:

    a) What do you expect the prosecutor will say about the statement and the informant Reese in Closing Argument?

    b) Draft the cross-examination of Reese on the points you feel are important.

    c) What would you expect the defense to say in Closing Argument?

3. What legal grounds does the defense have to suppress the statement?

4. Is there any other factual information the defense may wish to obtain by discovery in preparing for the motion to suppress? Why?

5. What are the pivotal facts (good or bad) for the defense? How will the defense deal with the bad facts?

6. What will be the prosecution's position? What are the weaknesses in this position? How would you expect the prosecution to deal with such weaknesses?

EXERCISES.
1. *Defense Attorneys*. Plan a motion to suppress the alleged confession, brainstorming a full adversary analysis:

   a) witnesses;
   b) direct and cross-examinations; and
   c) arguments to the Court.

VII. TOM KATSINSKI TALKS TO AN INFORMANT

Is there any other factual information the defense may wish to obtain by discovery in preparing for the motion to suppress? Why?

5. What are the pivotal facts (good or bad) for the defense? How will the defense deal with the bad facts?

6. What will be the prosecution's position? What are the weaknesses in this position? How would you expect the prosecution to deal with such weaknesses?

EXERCISES

1. Defense Attorneys: Plan a motion to suppress the alleged confession, brainstorming a full adversary analysis:

a) all witnesses;
b) direct and cross-examinations; and
c) arguments to the court.

CHAPTER VII
The Identification of
Thomas Katsinski

VII.1. James Dailey Identifies "T.C." Through a Photograph

In his confession, James Dailey indicated that he would be able to identify "Tom Cat" if he ever saw him. Subsequently, Dailey was shown the photograph of three men that was seized from the cabin at "The Rancho." Dailey identified the one whose shirt bore the initials "T.C." as the man he knew as "Tom Cat." This led the police to Thomas Katsinski. James is now prepared to testify for the State and identify Katsinski in court.

In this assignment, you will assess the legal significance of this photo display and identification from the perspectives of prosecutor and defense attorney. [Issues of TAINT are dealt with elsewhere in these materials.]

Review Appendices X and DD in CASEFILE and pages which your instructor will assign in your Coursebook.

PLANNING QUESTIONS.
1. Assess the impact to the prosecution if Dailey is not permitted to identify Katsinski in court.

2. One final checklist. List all the factors which (in theory) could make a photo identification procedure "suggestive" ...

3. Assume you are in a jurisdiction where the court decides the admissibility of the out-of-court and in-court identification separately. The court suppresses the photo ID, but not the in-court ID. How would that affect the prosecution's case against Katsinski? What tactical position would that leave the defense in?

4. What are the main points the prosecution will raise in arguing that the photo display was not unconstitutional (i.e., did not lead to an irreparable chance of misidentification)?

5. What are the main points the defense will raise arguing that it was unconstitutional?

6. Prior to the hearing, will you do any further investigation? What (specifically) will you seek (e.g., interview James Dailey, go to the scene, etc.)? Why?

7. Assuming the trial court rules that James Dailey may both testify about his photo identification of Katsinski and identify Katsinski in court, what do you expect the defense will say about this testimony in Closing Argument?

8. *Defense Attorneys*. You are talking to James Dailey's mom. You believe your client, Tom Katsinski, is innocent. You have the transcript of James's confession and believe you can convince Ms. Dailey that Detective Tevens badly used and misled her son. Can you do this in the hopes that Ms. Dailey will influence James to be less certain about his identification, or at least about your client's role in the case?

EXERCISES.
Your instructor will divide you into prosecution or defense.

Prosecutors and Defense Attorneys. Be prepared to argue to the trial court regarding whether the photo identification should be suppressed on due process grounds of suggestibility.

CHAPTER VIII
The Question of Who Can Complain and What Really Matters

VIII.1. A Surprising Route to the Suppression of the Tapes in the Trailer

The *defense* obviously views the tapes found in the trailer as the most serious evidence against Katsinski. The defense is contemplating a motion to suppress the tapes based, among other grounds, on the following chain of ''taint'': Katsinski is illegally arrested at a demonstration → booking photo taken → Officer Seltzer sees Freely photo on police bulletin board → Seltzer matches face with previous mass arrest → finds booking photo → leads to address → police go to address to arrest Katsinski → find tapes.

In this assignment, you will take the role of defense counsel and do an adversary evaluation of the chain(s) of taint involving the seizure of the tapes in the trailer.

Review Appendices X, Y, AA, BB, CC, DD, and EE in CASEFILE and pages which your instructor will assign in your Coursebook.

PLANNING QUESTIONS.
1. *Defense Attorneys*. What are the problems with your position? How will you deal with such problems?

2. What do you anticipate will be the prosecution's position? What are the weaknesses in this position? How do you expect the prosecution to deal with these weaknesses?

EXERCISES.
1. *Defense Attorneys*. Draft a one (1) page memo to your supervisor outlining your position for the upcoming suppression motion and the position you expect the *Prosecutor* will take. Be prepared to "sit down and discuss" your memo in person with your supervisor.

2. Besides the taint between the suggestive photo identification (due process) and the in-court ID, there are other, totally different chains of taint. Chart each such "chain" that leads to the discovery of the boxes in the trailer.

VIII.2. Who Can Argue What?

When all the dust settles, there are a number of defendants and each faces charges based on evidence obtained in a variety of searches, seizures, identifications, and interrogations. The defense attorneys would obviously like to suppress as much of this evidence as possible, but unless their clients have standing, they can't even raise the arguments.

In this assignment, you will take the role of defense attorney and analyze the standing of each defendant.

Review Appendices A, C, D, K, O, P, Q, R, T, V, Y, Z, AA, BB, DD, EE, and HH in CASEFILE and pages which your instructor will assign in your Coursebook.

<u>EXERCISES</u>.

1. *Defense Attorneys*. Provide your supervisor with a memo outlining for each defendant (which your instructor tells you to analyze):

   a) the pieces of evidence harmful to that defendant;
   b) the police/government action(s) which led to obtaining the evidence;
   c) a theory of standing for the defendant as to each of these police/-government actions;
   d) any problem(s) with your theory and how you propose to deal with the problem(s).

CHAPTER IX
The Case Proceeds Towards Trial

IX.1. Thomas Katsinski Seeks Discovery

Thomas Katsinski's attorney is now planning strategy for discovery. Katsinski has maintained that he had no part in, or even knowledge of, the conspiracy or any illegal activity. Jardine is his neighbor, and they sometimes go to a movie or lunch together. He has been out to "The Rancho" once for a barbecue. Freely is on Katsinki's bowling team. Other than that, he insists that he has never even met any of the other defendants. Finally, he maintains that the boxes of tapes in the trailer were already there when he moved in.

In this assignment, you will take the role of counsel for Katsinski and plan (1) general discovery and (2) a strategy for seeking the identity of the confidential informant referred to in the affidavit for the search warrant.

Review Appendices A, C, D, E, Q, R, V, Y, and Z in CASEFILE and pages which your instructor will assign in your Coursebook.

PLANNING QUESTIONS.
1. What general items of discovery will you seek from the prosecution and/or police?

2. Why (in terms of your theory of Katsinski's defense) are you seeking this information? [Alternatively, how could it help your case or lead to information that will help your case?]

3. Do you anticipate that the prosecution will object to any of your requests? If so, how will you respond?

4. Focusing on the request for the informant's identity ...

    a) Summarize the law regarding overcoming the governmental informant privilege.

    b) Can you meet this standard? Explain.

    c) What response do you anticipate from the prosecution? How will you answer?

    d) As a practical matter, what helpful information could you reasonably obtain from the informant?

e) Imagine the following. You know that if you are successful and convince the Court to order the prosecution to reveal the informant's identity, the prosecution will dismiss the case against your client rather than turn over the informant. You further believe that you have reasonable legal grounds to seek the informant's identity. The problem is that your client tells you that he already knows who the informant is. Under these circumstances, may you ethically file your motion to compel the identity of the informant?

EXERCISES.
Attorneys for defendant Katsinski. Draft an affidavit (or declaration) detailing why you are entitled to the name of the confidential informant.

IX.2. The Prosecution Seeks Discovery From Katsinski

The prosecution has just sent the following interrogatory to Thomas Katsinski's attorney:

INTERROGATORY #1

Please provide the current location of all correspondence or other documents sent between Thomas Katsinski and Gilbert Jardine. The State stipulates that, for purposes of trial, a response to this interrogatory shall not be considered in any way to be an admission by defendant Katsinski that he was aware of the existence, content, or location of any such correspondence or documents. Nor shall it be an admission of the authenticity of such correspondence or documents; nor will the fact that defendant produced these documents be used in any manner in the State's case in chief.

In this assignment, you will evaluate how to respond to this request as attorney for defendant Katsinski.

Review Appendix A in CASEFILE and pages which your instructor will assign in your Coursebook.

EXERCISES.
Attorneys for defendant Katsinski. Brainstorm your strategy for responding to this request.

CHAPTER X
The Pre-trial Motions Roll In

X.1. Frone and Stern Move to Sever

Boyd Stern, who has been charged with illegal possession of the single tape found in the Camaro, but not conspiracy, has been joined for trial with Katsinski, Jardine, Freely, Bean, Lumus, Klein, and Broil. His DWI case has been severed from the illegal possession of the cassette tape charge, and his attorney now seeks to further sever his tape case from that of Katsinski et al.

Miller Frone is set for a single trial in which he will be charged with possession of marijuana and illegal possession of the cassette tape found in the pat search at the airport. (He lost his suppression motion.) His attorney now seeks separate trials on each charge.

In this assignment, you will analyze the two defense motions for severance from the perspectives of both prosecution and defense.

Review Appendices A, B, C, D, E, R, T, V, Y, Z, AA, and BB in CASEFILE and pages which your instructor will assign in your Coursebook.

PLANNING QUESTIONS.
1. What standards guide the Court in evaluating a motion for mandatory or permissive severance of (a) counts (b) defendants?

2. As to Boyd Stern ...

   a) What are the pivotal facts (good or bad) for his position?

   b) What will his attorney argue?

c) What will the prosecution respond?

d) Imagine you are defense counsel and can obtain a declaration from Gil Jardine that he would testify favorably for Stern (without specifically stating what he would say) if Stern's case is severed and follows his own. Is this useful for your severance motion? Why? Do you care if it's truthful? How can you know?

3. As to Miller Frone ...

a) What will the defense argue?

b) What will the prosecution respond?

c) *Defense attorneys.* Imagine you lose the motion. At trial, the judge gives an instruction that the jury must consider each of the two charges as if they were separate trials. Now, consider the grounds on which you sought severance. How could you use this same theme in Closing Argument to the jury?

<u>EXERCISES</u>.
Your instructor will first divide you into prosecution or defense, and then between the *Frone* and *Stern* cases.

1. *Defense Attorneys and Prosecutors in the <u>Frone</u> case*:

   a) Using your casebook as your "library," draft a (2-page) memo to the court arguing your respective positions on the defense motion for severance of counts.
   b) Prepare to argue your position to the Court.

2. *Defense Attorneys and Prosecutors in the <u>Stern</u> case*:

   a) Using your casebook as your "library," draft a (2-page) memo to the court arguing your respective positions on the defense motion for severance of defendants.
   b) Prepare to argue your position to the Court.

X.2. Examining the Consequences of a Successful Licensing Hearing

Consistent with state law, Boyd Stern's driver's license was seized by Officer Smith and temporarily revoked by the Department of Licensing (D.O.L.) pending the outcome of his criminal trial for Driving While Intoxicated. Under § 42.030(c) of the state code, Stern appealed the revocation of his license to the D.O.L. on the statutory grounds that the officer did not have probable cause to arrest him for DWI. A hearing was set before a Commissioner of the D.O.L. Under § 42.030(d), Stern had the burden at this hearing of establishing a lack of probable cause by a "preponderance of the evidence." Present at the hearing were Stern, Stern's attorney, and Officer Smith. Officer Smith testified under oath and was cross-examined by Stern's attorney. At the conclusion of the hearing, the Commissioner found that the officer lacked probable cause to arrest Stern for DWI, and ordered Stern's license

CHAPTER X. THE PRE-TRIAL MOTIONS ROLL IN

reinstated. The Commissioner indicated that his decision was based on a "credibility determination."

In this assignment, you will assess the possible significance of these events for Stern's criminal case from both the prosecution and defense perspectives.

Review Appendices A and C in CASEFILE and pages which your instructor will assign in your Coursebook.

<u>PLANNING QUESTIONS</u>.
1. What legal principle(s) of possible significance to Stern's (1) DWI case and (2) possession of bootleg tapes case, are implicated by the results of the licensing hearing?

2. *Prosecutors and Defense Attorneys.* What are the pivotal facts (good or bad) for your respective sides? Why?

<u>EXERCISES</u>.
Your instructor will divide you into prosecution or defense.

> *Prosecutors and Defense Attorneys.* Using the results of the licensing hearing, the defense has calendared motions to dismiss both the DWI and bootleg cases against Stern for lack of probable cause. Each side prepare to argue your position to the Court.

80

X.3. Lumus and Katsinski Move to Dismiss for Time Delays

After his arrest at "The Rancho," Kevin Lumus was held in custody along with Jardine, Freely, Klein, and Bean for two days. At this time, the prosecution was not prepared to file charges, and the defendants were released. Lumus then went home to the southern part of the state and heard nothing more about the case until two years later when he was arrested on an out-standing bench warrant that police discovered while doing a routine warrant check during a traffic stop for a taillight violation. Apparently, after the Indictment in the case was filed, a summons was sent to Lumus but, because Officer Morris had inverted Lumus's zip code when he drafted the arrest report of 11/27/Y-1, the summons was return-stamped "Undeliverable as Addressed." When Lumus failed to make his first court appearance, a bench warrant was issued. The state made no other efforts to locate him. Lumus claims that he is a horse trainer and was only on "The Rancho" that day to see about buying a cutting horse for a client, Mr. Harvey Pisnell. Unfortunately, Mr. Pisnell is currently on a trek in Nepal and cannot be reached.

Thomas Katsinski was also released shortly after his initial arrest and did not appear in Court until after the Indictment. Katsinski claims that his regular postman, Edgar Quinn, could testify that the boxes of tapes were already in the trailer the day Katsinski moved in. Quinn had previously had a brief conversation with Gil Jardine when Jardine occupied the trailer, and remembered commenting on how crowded the boxes made the trailer. The problem is that two weeks before the Indictment came out, Quinn had a stroke. As a result, he gets easily confused about time sequences and events, and although he still claims to remember seeing the boxes of tapes when Jardine occupied the trailer, he is mentally impaired to the extent that it is obvious to any observer.

The prosecutor, on the other hand, did not seek an earlier indictment for a number of reasons. Initially, the prosecution was trying to "develop sources" (i.e., make deals with lower-level members of the conspiracy to testify against higher-ups). These negotiations went on for a while and eventually fell through. Also, the prosecution had "more important" cases to prepare and present to a grand jury that was already somewhat backlogged.

In this assignment, you will do an adversary analysis of this information.

Review Appendices A, X, Y, CC, DD, EE, FF, II, JJ, and KK in CASEFILE and pages which your instructor will assign in your Coursebook.

<u>PLANNING QUESTIONS</u>.
1. Summarize the law that circumscribes the significance of the above facts in (a) Lumus's and (b) Katsinski's cases.

2. Focusing on Lumus ...

    a) What are the pivotal facts (good or bad) for each side?

    b) What will the defense argue?

    c) What will the prosecution respond?

3. Focusing on Katsinski ...

    a) What are the pivotal facts (good or bad) for each side?

b) What will the defense argue?

c) What will the prosecution argue?

EXERCISES.
Your instructor will divide you into prosecution and defense, and then assign you to the *Lumus* or *Katsinski* cases.

1. *Prosecutors and Defense Attorneys in the Lumus case.*

   a) Meet separately and plan your approach to this information.
   b) Be prepared to argue your positions to the Court.

2. *Prosecutors and Defense attorneys in the Katsinski case.*

   a) Meet separately and plan your approach to this information.
   b) Be prepared to argue your positions to the Court.

STATE *v. KATSINSKI et al.*

CASEFILE

[Appendices]

CASEFILE INDEX

IN THE SUPERIOR COURT OF THE STATE OF CASCADIA
IN AND FOR THE COUNTY OF NETTLE

STATE OF CASCADIA,	)	NO. *Y-1*-9-01621-2
Plaintiff,	)	
vs.	)	
	)	INFORMATION
THOMAS L. KATSINSKI, GILBERT	)	
J. JARDINE, WILLIAM J. BEAN,	)	
BOYD C. STERN, RALPH FREELY,	)	
RACHEL R. KLEIN, KEVIN M. LUMUS,	)	
EDWARD G. BROIL,	)	
Defendants.	)	

COUNT I

I, KATHRYN Q. McMANIS, Prosecuting Attorney for the County of Nettle, in the name and authority of the State of Cascadia, do accuse that on or about 6/Y-2 to 11/27/Y-1, THOMAS L. KATSINSKI, GILBERT J. JARDINE, EDWARD G. BROIL, RALPH FREELY, WILLIAM J. BEAN, KEVIN M. LUMUS, RACHEL R. KLEIN, and uncharged co-conspirator JAMES E. DAILEY did violate 9.777, CONSPIRACY, in that they did together PLAN, SCHEME, and AGREE TO DUPLICATE, STORE, AND DISTRIBUTE UNAUTHORIZED DUPLICATED COPYRIGHTED MATERIAL; to wit: cassette tapes of live concerts.

Overt Act #1. Sometime between 6/Y-2 and 11/27/Y-1, members of the conspiracy rented P. O. Box #609 in the Nettletown main post office for purposes of transmitting moneys and communication.

Overt Act #2. Sometime between 6/Y-2 and 11/27Y-1, members of the conspiracy painted the buildings at "The Rancho" camouflage colors and located duplicating and packaging machines.

Overt Act #3. From on or about 1/Y-1 to 9/Y-1, GILBERT J. JARDINE purchased over $20,000 worth of recording equipment.

INFORMATION
Page 1 of 3

APPENDIX A

<u>Overt Act #4</u>. On or about 6/Y-2, EDWARD G. BROIL recruited JAMES E. DAILEY to sell and distribute bootleg cassette tapes.

<u>Overt Act #5</u>. On or about 9/8/Y-1, GILBERT J. JARDINE rented a Mercury Cougar and Chevrolet Camaro to transport tapes and otherwise assist the conspiracy.

<u>Overt Act #6</u>. On or about 11/27/Y-1, WILLIAM J. BEAN transported boxes of bootleg tapes in his Pontiac Firebird.

<u>Overt Act #7</u>. Sometime prior to 1/29/Y-0, THOMAS L. KATSINSKI stored cartons of bootleg tapes in a Silverglide trailer near his home.

COUNT II

I, KATHRYN Q. McMANIS, Prosecuting Attorney for the County of Nettle, in the name and authority of the State of Cascadia, do accuse that on or about 11/27/Y-1, GILBERT J. JARDINE, EDWARD G. BROIL, RALPH FREELY, KEVIN M. LUMUS, and RACHEL R. KLEIN did violate 15.006(d), POSSESSION OF UNAUTHORIZED DUPLICATED COPYRIGHTED MATERIAL, in that they did knowingly have possession, custody and/or control of such materials; to wit: boxes of cassette tapes of various concerts, said boxes being located at premises known as "The Rancho."

COUNT III

I, KATHRYN Q. McMANIS, Prosecuting Attorney for the County of Nettle, in the name and by the authority of the State of Cascadia, do accuse that on or about 11/27/Y-1, WILLIAM J. BEAN did violate 15.006(d), POSSESSION OF UNAUTHORIZED DUPLICATED COPYRIGHTED MATERIAL, in that he did knowingly have possession, custody, and/or control of such materials; to wit: boxes of cassette tapes of various concerts, said boxes being located in the trunk of a Pontiac Firebird, license #BUH 707, while the car was registered to, and being driven by, BEAN.

COUNT IV

I, KATHRYN Q. McMANIS, Prosecuting Attorney for the County of Nettle, in the name and by the authority of the State of Cascadia, do accuse that on or about 1/29/Y-0,

INFORMATION
Page 2 of 3

THOMAS L. KATSINSKI did violate 15.006(d), POSSESSION OF UNAUTHORIZED DUPLICATED COPYRIGHTED MATERIALS, in that he did knowingly have possession, control, and/or custody of such materials; to wit: boxes of cassette tapes of various concerts, said boxes being located in a Silverglide trailer being occupied by KATSINSKI at the time and being located next to his home.

COUNT V

I, KATHRYN Q. McMANIS, Prosecuting Attorney for the County of Nettle, in the name and authority of the State of Cascadia, do accuse that on or about 9/9/Y-1, BOYD C. STERN did violated 15.006(d), POSSESSION OF UNAUTHORIZED DUPLICATED COPYRIGHTED MATERIALS, in that he did knowingly have possession, control, and/or custody of such materials; to wit: a cassette tape of a concert, said tape being found on the floor of a Chevrolet Camaro STERN was driving at the time.

DATED this 30th day of July, Y-0.

Kathryn Q McManis
KATHRYN Q. McMANIS
Prosecuting Attorney in and for said
County and State

INFORMATION
Page 3 of 3

2

3 IN THE SUPERIOR COURT OF THE STATE OF CASCADIA
IN AND FOR THE COUNTY OF NETTLE

4

5 STATE OF CASCADIA,   )
            Plaintiff,   )   NO. *Y-1*-8-00316-2

6   vs.   )
)   INFORMATION

7 MILLER P. FRONE,   )
            Defendant.   )

8 _____)

9 COUNT I

10   I, KATHRYN Q. McMANIS, Prosecuting Attorney for the County of Nettle, in the

11 name and authority of the State of Cascadia, do accuse that on or about 9/9/Y-1, MILLER P.

12 FRONE did violate 15.006(d), POSSESSION OF UNAUTHORIZED DUPLICATED

13 COPYRIGHTED MATERIALS, in that he did knowingly have possession, control, and/or

14 custody of said materials; to wit: a cassette tape of a concert found on his person.

15 COUNT II

16   I, KATHRYN Q. McMANIS, Prosecuting Attorney for the County of Nettle, in the

17 name and authority of the State of Cascadia, do accuse that on or about 9/9/Y-2, MILLER P.

18 FRONE did violate 9.514(c), POSSESSION OF A CONTROLLED SUBSTANCE, in that he

19 did knowingly have possession, control, and/or custody of such controlled substance; to wit:

20 three (3) hand-rolled cigarettes containing MARIJUANA found on his person.

21   DATED this 5th day of March, Y-0.

22   *Kathryn Q. McManis*

23   KATHRYN Q. McMANIS
                             Prosecuting Attorney in and for said

24   County and State

25

26

27

28

INFORMATION
Page 1 of 1

APPENDIX B

ARREST REPORT

AGENCY:

[X] NPD [ ] TFTF

OTHER: _____

Page 1 of 4

1	Public Disclosure Act		

2 Arrest	✓ 3 Vehicle	4 Juvenile	8 Report Name/Offense
5 Property	6 Medical	7 Domestic Viol	DWI / POSSESSION OF MARIJUANA

9 Type of Premise (For vehicles, state where parked.)	10 Entry Point	11 Method

12 Weapon /Tool/Force Used	13 Date Reported 9.9.4-1	14 Time Reported 1545	15 Date Occurrence —	16 Time Occurrence —	17 Day of Week

18 Location of: Incident Address [X] NETTLETOWN AIRPORT		19 Census	20 Dist.

PERSONS/BUSINESS INVOLVED

CODE	C (Person Reporting Complaint)	V (Victim)	W (Witness)	P (Parent)	VB (Victim Business)	O (Other)

21 Code	22 NAME: Last	First	Middle (Maiden)	23 Race/Sex	24 Date of Birth	25 Home Phone
26 DPA	27 ADDRESS: Street	City	State	Zip	28 Place of Employment/School	29 Business Phone
21 Code	22 NAME: Last	First	Middle (Maiden)	23 Race/Sex	24 Date of Birth	25 Home Phone
26 DPA	27 ADDRESS: Street	City	State	Zip	28 Place of Employment/School	29 Business Phone
21 Code	22 NAME: Last	First	Middle (Maiden)	23 Race/Sex	24 Date of Birth	25 Home Phone
26 DPA	27 ADDRESS: Street	City	State	Zip	28 Place of Employment/School	29 Business Phone

[ ] Additional persons on Report Continuation Sheet (People) Form No. Z-556

CODE:	A (Arrest)	S (Suspect)	SV (Suspect Verified)	R (Runaway)	M (Missing Person)	I (Institutional Impact)

PERSON NUMBER 1

30 Code	31 NAME: Last	First	Middle (Maiden)	32 Home Phone	33 Business Phone
A	(S#1) STERN	BOYD	C.		

34 ADDRESS: Street	City	State	Zip	35 Occupation	36 Place of Employment/School	37 Relation to Victim
26307 MIDVALE DR	NETTLETOWN		00071	PAINTER	SELF-EMPLOYED	

38 Date of Birth	39 Race	40 Sex	41 Height	42 Weight/Build	43 Hair	44 Eyes	45 Clothing, Scars, marks, Tattoos, Peculiarities, A.K.A.
3|17|4-33	C	M	5'7"	152 lbs	brn	brn	

46 [X] Booked [ ] Cited	Number	47 Charge Details (Include Ordinance or R.C.W. Number) 10.037 (DWI)

PERSON NUMBER 2

30 Code	31 NAME: Last	First	Middle (Maiden)	32 Home Phone	33 Business Phone
A	(S#2) FRONE	MILLER	P		

34 ADDRESS: Street	City	State	Zip	35 Occupation	36 Place of Employment/School	37 Relation to Victim
71 GREENWOOD LN	NETTLETOWN		00070	PAINTER	SELF-EMPLOYED	

38 Date of Birth	39 Race	40 Sex	41 Height	42 Weight/Build	43 Hair	44 Eyes	45 Clothing, Scars, marks, Tattoos, Peculiarities, A.K.A.
5|21|4-34	C	M	5'11"	175 lbs.	MED. BRN	BRN	MOUSTACHE

46 [X] Booked [ ] Cited	Number	47 Charge Details (Include Ordinance or R.C.W. Number) 9.514(c) POSSESS. of Controlled Substance/marijuana

[ ] Additional persons on Report Continuation Sheet (People) Form No. Z-556   Juvenile Arrests - Block No. 109 MUST Be completed

VEHICLE

48 Stolen	49 Victim	50 Impound	✓ 54 License No.	55 Lic/State	56 Lic/Year	57 Lic/Type	58 Vin.
51 Recovery	52 Suspect	53 Hold	LL3 617		4-1		

59 Year	60 Make	61 Model	62 Body Style	63 Color	64 Peculiarities	65 Hold Requested by/For
4-10	FORD	CAMARO		WHITE		

66 Ori. & Case No.	67 Registered Owner: Name	Address	City	State	Zip	68 Home Phone
	AJAX RENTAL WRECKS	137 MAIN ST	NETTLETOWN		00074	627-2301

69 Condition [ ] Drivable [ ] Not Drivable	[ ] Stripped [ ] Wrecked	70 Inventory

70 Inventory (Continued)	71 Tow Co. & Signature

72 Enter	73 Date	74 Time	75 WACIC	76 LESA	77 Initial	78 Release Info	79 Date	80 Time	81 Release No.	82 Releasing Authority
83 Clear	84	85	86	87	88	89 Owner Notified	90	91	92 Operator's Name	

93 Signature & I.D. No. of Reporting Officer(s) K. Smith (#926)	94 Approval	95 Distribution Excp.

REPORT PROCESSING (Records Personnel Only)	DISTRIBUTION: DATE _____ BY _____ INDEXED: DATE _____ BY _____	Microfilmed Initials _____	Filed Initials _____

C3:\C\P\\POLICE.RPT

APPENDIX C

NARRATIVE:

At 1545 hours, RO and partner Officer Dobbins (Badge #127) were at the Nettletown Airport (NTL) in response to call from unnamed source concerning a drug shipment. Source indicated that two white males in a Y-10 white Chevrolet Camaro were going to pick up marijuana from unknown person arriving on Eastwinds Airlines. Officers observed Suspect #1, later identified as BOYD STERN, drive a white Y-10 Chevrolet Camaro to the door of Eastwinds Airlines and drop off Suspect #2, later identified as MILLER FRONE. As the Camaro pulled away from the curb, the driver failed to signal and then pulled in the path of a courtesy van, causing the van to slam on its brakes to avoid a collision. The Camaro then began to weave in its lane, traveling from the fog line to the center divider line and back several times. Officers proceeded to follow and were about to effect a traffic stop when the Camaro pulled into the "minimum one week" NTL Airport parking lot. Officers followed into the lot, where the Camaro had secured a parking space, and contacted Suspect #1, who identified himself as Boyd Stern. RO noticed that S#1 had difficulty removing his identification from his wallet and was talking in a disjointed, rambling manner. RO did not smell any alcohol, but from S#1's behavior and the previous driving observed, RO suspected that S#1 was under the influence of some drug.

While S#1 was ordered out of the vehicle and asked to take the field sobriety tests (FSTs), my partner radioed Airport Security Guard Rosten to detain and question S#2, the man S#1 had dropped off, as to possible involvement with drugs. In order to have a good level surface and a place safe from traffic for the FSTs, RO located a spot approximately 150 feet from S#1's vehicle. S#1 at first agreed to perform FSTs. The first test required saying the ABCs. S#1 stopped after "F", started laughing, and began again from the start. He then finished, but left out "Q." When I pointed this out to him, he indicated that "Q" was not a very important letter and began laughing uncontrollably. RO then asked S#1 to perform the "walk and turn" balancing test. S#1 refused and refused to take any other FSTs.

S#1 was then placed under arrest for Driving Under the Influence of Intoxicants, handcuffed on the spot, and placed in the back of the patrol car. Officer Dobbins then did a search of the passenger compartment where he observed a small black object on the floor near the front passenger's seat. Officer Dobbins retrieved the object which was revealed to be a cassette tape recording. The tape was placed in an evidence bag and transported to the evidence room. Because S#1 was intoxicated and thus unable to drive, and because there was no one else available to drive the Camaro, RO had vehicle towed to police garage for safekeeping.

As we were about to transport S#1 to the station, we received a call from Airport Security Guard Rosten indicating that he had found three marijuana cigarettes on the person of S#2, MILLER FRONE, and was holding S#2 for Nettletown Police. (Report of Airport Security Guard Rosten attached.) We proceeded to Eastwinds Terminal where Rosten had S#2 in custody. After talking to Rosten and inspecting the three cigarettes, which plainly contained marijuana, S#2 was placed under arrest for possession of marijuana and transported to station with S#1. The three marijuana cigarettes, a cassette tape, and hand-drawn map were secured for evidence and transported to evidence room.

During routine booking search of S#1 at jail, RO found postcard from person named "Gil." Message on card states, "The stuff is ready at Rancho for you to pick up ... real hiiiigh fidelity!!!" Postcard placed in evidence with cassette tape found in search of car.

PROPERTY REPORT

AGENCY   NPD ☒   TFTF O   OTHER _____   DATE 9-9-4-1

PROP ROOM USE ONLY	PAGE 4 of 5

TYPE OF CRIME
DwI

☒ EVIDENCE   O FOUND
O SAFEKEEPING   O OWNER UNKNOWN

LABORATORY WORK REQUIRED: YES _____

RELATED CASE NO.

CENSUS   DIST.

PROPERTY OBTAINED FROM: ADDRESS   PHONE

V I C T I M	LAST NAME	FIRST	MIDDLE	S U B J E C T	LAST NAME	FIRST	MIDDLE
	STREET ADDRESS	CITY	PHONE		STERN	BOYD	C
					STREET ADDRESS 26301 Midvale Dr.	CITY Nettletown	PHONE

PROPERTY INVENTORY					PROPERTY ROOM USE ONLY	
ITEM NO.	PROPERTY DESCRIPTION	QTY	SERIAL NO.	WA NOC	LOCATION	RECEIPT NO.
1	Postcard	1				
2	Cassette Tape	1				

PROPERTY SUBMITTED BY: K.Smith (#926) _____ UNIT NO: _____ DATE: 9-9-4-1
ADDITIONAL DESCRIPTIONS OR COMMENTS:

IOP ROOM USE ONLY	PROPERTY RECEIVED: METHOD _____ BY: _____ DATE: _____
	PROPERTY INVENTORIED BY: _____ UNIT: _____ DATE: _____

C2\CJ\PRP-RPT.FRM

PROPERTY REPORT

AGENCY NPD ☒ TFTF ○ OTHER _____ **DATE** 9-9-4-1

PROP ROOM USE ONLY	I PAGE
	15065

TYPE OF CRIME Possession of Marijuana

☒ EVIDENCE ○ FOUND

○ SAFEKEEPING ○ OWNER UNKNOWN

LABORATORY WORK REQUIRED: YES ✓
Check for Marijuana

RELATED CASE NO.

CENSUS	DIST.

PROPERTY OBTAINED FROM: **ADDRESS** **PHONE**

V I C T I M	LAST NAME	FIRST	MIDDLE
	STREET ADDRESS	CITY	PHONE

S U B J E C T	LAST NAME	FIRST	MIDDLE
	Krone	Miller	P.
	STREET ADDRESS 71 Greenwood Ln	CITY Nettletown	PHONE

PROPERTY INVENTORY

ITEM NO.	PROPERTY DESCRIPTION	QTY	SERIAL NO.	WA NOC	LOCATION	RECEIPT NO.
1	3 hand-rolled cigs (suspect marijuana)					
2	Cassette Tape ("Slime" Concert)					
3	Hand-drawn map					

PROPERTY SUBMITTED BY: K. Smith (#936   **UNIT NO:** _____ **DATE:** 9-9-4-1

ADDITIONAL DESCRIPTIONS OR COMMENTS:

IOP ROOM USE ONLY	
	PROPERTY RECEIVED: METHOD _____ BY: _____ DATE: _____
	PROPERTY INVENTORIED BY: _____ UNIT: _____ DATE: _____

C2\CV\PRP-RPT.FRM

DATE: 09/09/Y-1   TIME: 1555 hours

LOCATION: Nettletown Airport (Eastwinds Airlines Lounge)

ASSIGNMENT: Airport Security

REPORTED BY: Rosten, Airport Security

SUBJECT: Miller P. Frone   DOB: 05/21/Y-34
           71 Greenwood Ln.
           Nettletown, Cascadia 00070

INCIDENT: found the hand-rolled marijuana cigarettes on subject in pat-search; turned over to Nettletown Police dept.

NARRATIVE:

At 1555 hours I was on duty in the Eastwinds Airline terminal when I received a call from Nettletown police officer Smith to stop and question in relation to possible drug activity a WMA, mid-thirties, who had just been dropped off at the terminal by a white Y-10 Chevrolet Camaro.

I located a WMA, mid-thirties, fitting the description of the suspect given by Nettletown Police, and requested identification. The suspect, whose license indicated that his name was MILLER FRONE, complied and subsequently agreed to accompany me to the security room where I ran his license through the AVEX 20 Computer. While waiting both for results from AVEX check and for a confirming call from Airport Police, and concerned for my safety being alone in a small room with a possible drug suspect, I pat-searched Frone. During pat search I felt a hard 2" x 4" object in Frone's right coat pocket and removed the object, fearing it might be a weapon. Because the object was wrapped in paper, I had to undo the paper to determine its nature. Inside was a plastic cassette tape with "Slime — 3/17/Y-2" written on the box. A closer look at the paper in which the tape had been wrapped revealed a hand-drawn map of what appeared to be the "Big Tree"

APPENDIX D

area. As I was handing the map and tape back to Frone, three hand-rolled cigarettes—one half-smoked—fell from the map. Upon inspection, I immediately recognized that the cigarettes contained marijuana.

Frone was handcuffed and held for Nettletown police who I radioed. Officers arrived in a few minutes and took Frone into custody. I also provided officers with the three marijuana cigarettes, as well as the map and cassette.

Supplemental REPORT
AGENCY:
[X] NPD [ ] TFTF

1				
Public Disclosure Act	OTHER: _____			Page 1 of 4

2 Arrest	✓	3 Vehicle	4 Juvenile	8 Report Name/Offense
5 Property		6 Medical	7 Domestic Viol	

9 Type of Premise (For vehicles, state where parked.)	10 Entry Point	11 Method

12 Weapon /Tool/Force Used	13 Date Reported 9.15.9-1	14 Time Reported 1115	15 Date Occurrence 9.10.4-1 4.15.4-1	16 Time Occurrence	17 Day of Week

18 Location of: Incident [ ] Address [ ]		19 Census	20 Dist.

PERSONS/BUSINESS INVOLVED

CODE	C (Person Reporting Complaint)	V (Victim)	W (Witness)	P (Parent)	VB (Victim Business)	O (Other)

21 Code	22 NAME: Last	First	Middle (Maiden)	23 Race/Sex	24 Date of Birth	25 Home Phone
26 DPA	27 ADDRESS: Street	City	State Zip	28 Place of Employment/School		29 Business Phone
21 Code	22 NAME: Last	First	Middle (Maiden)	23 Race/Sex	24 Date of Birth	25 Home Phone
26 DPA	27 ADDRESS: Street	City	State Zip	28 Place of Employment/School		29 Business Phone
21 Code	22 NAME: Last	First	Middle (Maiden)	23 Race/Sex	24 Date of Birth	25 Home Phone
26 DPA	27 ADDRESS: Street	City	State Zip	28 Place of Employment/School		29 Business Phone

[ ] Additional persons on Report Continuation Sheet (People) Form No. Z-556

PERSON NUMBER 1

CODE:	A (Arrest)	S (Suspect)	SV (Suspect Verified)	R (Runaway)	M (Missing Person)	I (Institutional Impact)

30 Code A	31 NAME: Last (S#1) STERN	First BOYD	Middle (Maiden) C.		32 Home Phone	33 Business Phone
34 ADDRESS: Street	City	State Zip	35 Occupation	36 Place of Employment/School		37 Relation to Victim
38 Date of Birth	39 Race	40 Sex	41 Height	42 Weight/Build	43 Hair	44 Eyes	45 Clothing, Scars, marks, Tattoos, Peculiarities, A.K.A.

46 [ ] Booked [ ] Cited	Number	47 Charge Details (Include Ordinance or R.C.W. Number) 10.037 (DWI)

PERSON NUMBER 2

30 Code A	31 NAME: Last (S#2) FRONE	First MILLER	Middle (Maiden) P.		32 Home Phone	33 Business Phone
34 ADDRESS: Street	City	State Zip	35 Occupation	36 Place of Employment/School		37 Relation to Victim
38 Date of Birth	39 Race	40 Sex	41 Height	42 Weight/Build	43 Hair	44 Eyes	45 Clothing, Scars, marks, Tattoos, Peculiarities, A.K.A.

46 [ ] Booked [ ] Cited	Number	47 Charge Details (Include Ordinance or R.C.W. Number) 9.514(c) (Possess. of marijuana)

[ ] Additional persons on Report Continuation Sheet (People) Form No. Z-556   Juvenile Arrests - Block No. 109 MUST Be completed

VEHICLE

48 Stolen	49 Victim	50 Impound	✓ 54 License No. LL3617 LL3204	55 Lic/State	56 Lic/Year 4-1	57 Lic/Type	58 Vin.
51 Recovery	52 Suspect	✓ 53 Hold					

59 Year 4-10 4-10	60 Make FORD MERCURY	61 Model CAMARO COUGAR	62 Body Style	63 Color WHITE BEIGE	64 Peculiarities	65 Hold Requested by/For NETTLETOWN PROSECUTOR

66 Ori. & Case No.	67 Registered Owner: Name AJAX RENTAL WRECKS	Address 137 MAIN ST	City NETTLETOWN	State	Zip 00074	68 Home Phone 627-2301

69 Condition [ ] Drivable [ ] Not Drivable [ ] Stripped [ ] Wrecked	70 Inventory SEE ATTACHED SHEET.

70 Inventory (Continued)	71 Tow Co. & Signature

72 Enter	73 Date	74 Time	75 WACIC	76 LESA	77 Initial	78 Release Info	79 Date	80 Time	81 Release No.	82 Releasing Authority
83 Clear	84	85	86	87	88	89 Owner Notified	90	91	92 Operator's Name	

93 Signature & I.D. No. of Reporting Officer(s) K Smith (#926)	94 Approval	95 Distribution Excp.

REPORT PROCESSING (Records Personnel Only)	DISTRIBUTION: DATE _____ BY _____ INDEXED: DATE _____ BY _____	Microfilmed Initials _____	Filed Initials _____

C3:\CP\\POLICE.RPT

APPENDIX E

NARRATIVE:

At 0945 hours an inventory of the Y-10 white Chevrolet Camaro driven by S#1 was conducted at the police garage for the safety and protection of both S#1 and the city of Nettletown. The trunk, which was locked, was opened by a lever on the floor next to the driver's seat. Inside the trunk was a locked briefcase. The briefcase, however, was easily opened by merely twisting a coin under the latches. Upon opening the briefcase, it was found to contain a Bank of NettleCard receipt and rental agreements for rental of two vehicles: the suspect Camaro, and a Y-10 beige Mercury Cougar. The receipts were both in the name of "Gilbert Jardine." Also in the briefcase, and paperclipped to the receipt for the Cougar, was a parking tag dated September 8 for the same "one week minimum" lot at the airport where we stopped the Camaro.

Based upon the initial unidentified caller concerning marijuana, the fact that S#1 was apparently intoxicated on drugs, the fact that S#2 was found in possession of marijuana, and the involvement of multiple rented vehicles, it was my belief that the Mercury Cougar might contain evidence of drug trafficking.

At my direction, several officers from the Nettletown Police Department took the rental receipt for the Cougar, along with the parking tag, and went out to the Nettletown Airport. They located the suspect Mercury Cougar with the help of the parking lot attendant. While the attendant watched, the officers tried unsuccessfully to gain entry to the trunk. They returned to their patrol vehicle and radioed for a locksmith and master keys.

Upon returning to suspect vehicle to wait for the locksmith, they found that the attendant, Regina Attenborough, had successfully unlocked the trunk, and removed and opened two cardboard boxes. The boxes contained over 2,000 of what appeared to be bootleg tapes of various alternative artists, including the Princess Die Band, Revolting Babysitters, the Nerds, Crashing Boors, Yech, etc.

PROPERTY REPORT

AGENCY NPD ☒ TFTF ○ OTHER_____ **DATE** 9-10-4-1

TYPE OF CRIME
DWI

PROP ROOM USE ONLY	PAGE
1 30,4	

☒ EVIDENCE ○ FOUND

○ SAFEKEEPING ○ OWNER UNKNOWN

LABORATORY WORK REQUIRED: YES _____

RELATED CASE NO.

CENSUS | DIST.

PROPERTY OBTAINED FROM: Camero #LL3-617-(Inventory)

ADDRESS

PHONE

	LAST NAME	FIRST	MIDDLE		LAST NAME	FIRST	MIDDLE
VICTIM				**SUBJECT**	STERN	BOYD	C
	STREET ADDRESS	CITY	PHONE		STREET ADDRESS	CITY	PHONE
					26307 Midvale Dr. Nettletown		

PROPERTY INVENTORY

ITEM NO.	PROPERTY DESCRIPTION	QTY	SERIAL NO.	WA NOC	PROPERTY ROOM USE ONLY LOCATION	RECEIPT NO.
1	Credit Card receipt for Car Rental - name: Gil Jardine					
2	Rental receipt (Camaro/Cougar) - name: Gil Jardine					
3	Parking receipt (NTL 'one week min." lot)					
4	Brown leather briefcase					

PROPERTY SUBMITTED BY: K. Smith (#926) **UNIT NO:** _____ **DATE:** 9-10-4-1

ADDITIONAL DESCRIPTIONS OR COMMENTS:

IOP ROOM USE ONLY				
	PROPERTY RECEIVED: METHOD _____	BY: _____	DATE: _____	
	PROPERTY INVENTORIED BY: _____	UNIT: _____	DATE: _____	

C2\CJ\PRP-RPT.FRM

PROPERTY REPORT

AGENCY   NPD ○   TFTF ☒   OTHER _____   DATE 9·18·Y·1

| PROP ROOM USE ONLY | PAGE 4 of 4 |

TYPE OF CRIME

UNK / SUSPECT TAPE FRAUD

☒ EVIDENCE   ○ FOUND

○ SAFEKEEPING   ○ OWNER UNKNOWN

LABORATORY WORK REQUIRED   YES ✓

INSPECTS TAPES -POSSIBLE FRAUD

| CENSUS | DIST |

RELATED CASE NO

PROPERTY OBTAINED FROM: MERCURY COUGAR # LL3209

ADDRESS

PHONE

| **V I C T I M** | LAST NAME | FIRST | MIDDLE | **S U B J E C T** | LAST NAME | FIRST | MIDDLE |
| | STREET ADDRESS | CITY | PHONE | | STREET ADDRESS | CITY | PHONE |

PROPERTY INVENTORY

ITEM NO.	PROPERTY DESCRIPTION	QTY	SERIAL NO.	WA VOC	LOCATION	RECEIPT NO.
1	Boxes Cassette Tapes of Concerts Approx 2,000 tapes in 2 Boxes					

PROPERTY ROOM USE ONLY

PROPERTY SUBMITTED BY: M. AUSTIN (#501)   UNIT NO: _____   DATE: 9·18·Y·1

ADDITIONAL DESCRIPTIONS OR COMMENTS:

| IOP ROOM USE ONLY | PROPERTY RECEIVED: METHOD _____ BY: _____ DATE: _____ |
| | PROPERTY INVENTORIED BY: _____ UNIT: _____ DATE: _____ |

C2\CU\PRP-RPT.FRM

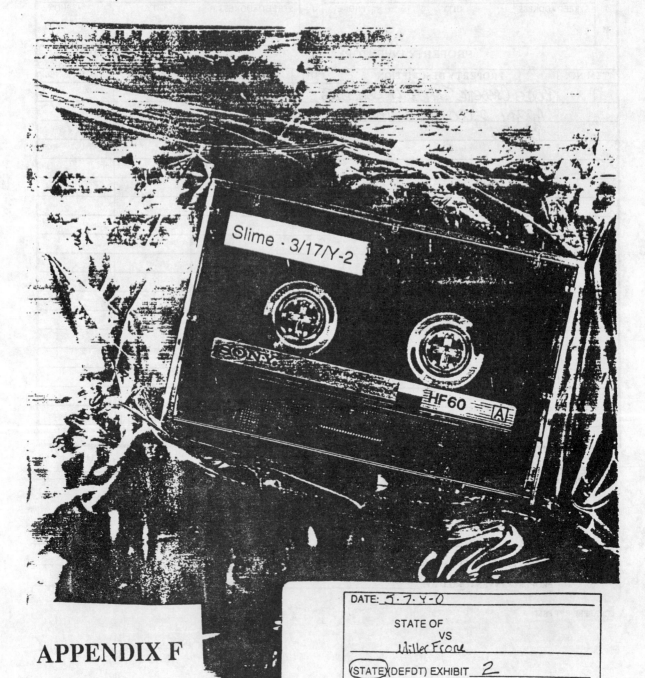

S.R. / Frone / 919/Y-7

Slime · 3/17/Y-2

SONY

HF 60 [A]

APPENDIX F

DATE: 5·7·Y-0

STATE OF
VS
Miller Frone

(STATE)(DEFDT) EXHIBIT   2

S.R. / Frone / 9/9/4-1

APPENDIX G

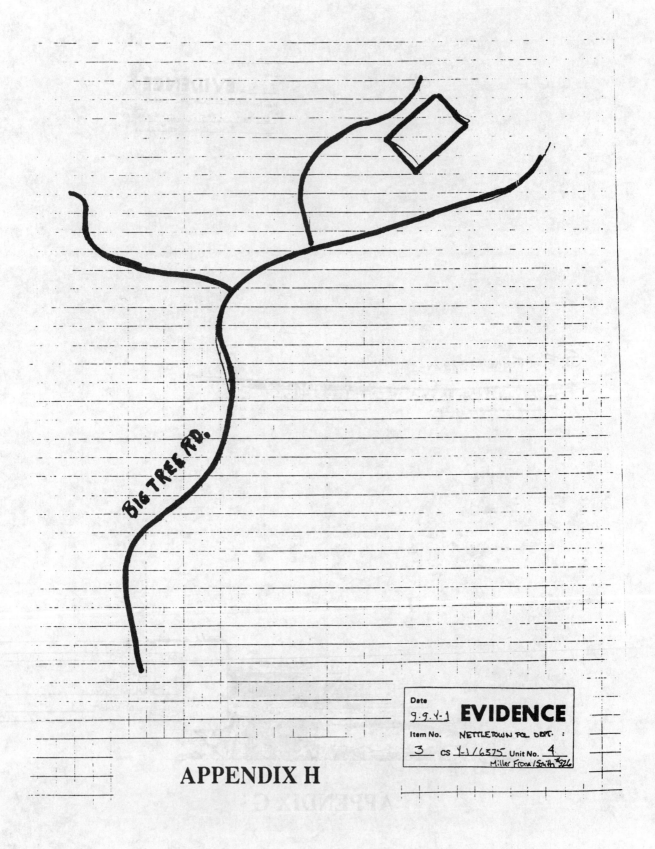

BIG TREE RD.

Date
9.9.Y.1 **EVIDENCE**

Item No.   NETTLETOWN POL. DEPT. :

3   CS Y-1/6375 Unit No. 4

Miller Frona/Smith #26

APPENDIX H

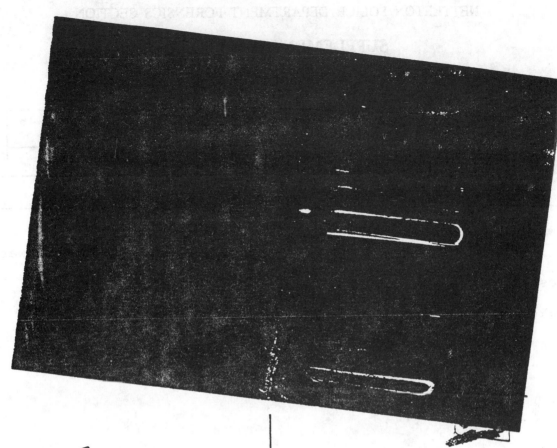

B-dude —

The stuff is ready
at Rancho for you to
pick up.... real hiiiigh
fidelity !!! "

Gil

**100,000 LBS. of
ICE and NEON**

Dale Chihuly in the Tacoma Dome

Mr. Boyd Stern
26307 Midvale Dr.
Nettletown
        OC071

Photo by Russell Johnson

APPENDIX I

SUPPLEMENTAL REPORT

Crime: Possible Possess. Of Controlled Substance	Case No.: Y-1-8-00316-2	CB: 436	District: 46
Victim: Unknown		Addr:	

_____**Narrative**_____

Three (3) hand-rolled cigarettes (one partially smoked) were tested as possibly containing marijuana. All three cigarettes tested positive for marijuana.

Page 1

Date: 10/19/Y-1	Technician: M. TAPPA #923		Approval
Distr. Date: _____	By: _____	Microfilmed: _____	By: _____
Indexed: _____	By: _____	Copy to: _____	

C2\C\J\FORENSIC.RPT

APPENDIX J

NETTLETOWN POLICE DEPARTMENT FORENSICS SECTION

LABORATORY REPORT

Crime: Possible Possess. Of Marijuana	Case No. Y-1-8-00316-2	CB: 436	District: 46
Victim: Unknown		Addr:	

Date of Lab Work: 10/19/Y-1

Examination Requested: PROCESS FOR POSSIBLE MARIJUANA CONTENTS.

Requested by:

_____ **Details** _____

Items Processed: ITEM #-1 Three (3) hand-rolled cigarettes.
One partially smoked.

Evidence Obtained: At Scene [ ]   Other Officer [ ]   Property Room [X]

Results/Remarks:

ITEM #1. Three (3) hand-rolled cigarettes. Were tested for
possible marijuana on 10/19/Y-1. Testing was positive for
marijuana.

See attached
MAR

Page 1

Date: 10/26/Y-1	Technician: M. TAPPA #923		Approval
Distr. Date: _____	By: _____	Microfilmed: _____	By: _____
Indexed: _____	By: _____	Copy to: _____	

C2\C\FORENSIC.LAB

MARIJUANA ANALYSIS REQUEST

Suspect's Name(s) *Miller P. Frone*

Case No. *4·1·8·003162*

Date Req. *9·15·4-1*

Req. By *NPD (Smith #926)*

Lab. No. _____

Evidence Item Numbers To Be Examined _____

Prosecutors Approval *CH* _____ Date _____

Forward to: [/] Identification [X] Crime Lab.

BELOW PORTION FOR IDENTIFICATION SECTION USE ONLY

MICROSCOPIC EXAMINATION

Leaf Material Color _____

Veins/Serrations _____/_____

Cystolithic Hairs _____*X*_____ (top of leaf)

Nonglandular (simple) hair _____ (bottom)

CHEMICAL TEST (Duquenois-Levine)

Violet color in aqueous phase _____*X*_____

Violet color transfers to chloroform phase _____*X*_____

_____

On *10·19* 19*4-1* the material tested [X] was: [ ] was not found to be marijuana. Net weight of green vegetable material *1 (approx.)* grams.

The tests were completed by *M. Tappa* No. *923*, a graduate of the Crime Laboratory Marijuana Leaf Identification Course. Total tests conducted to date *536*.

The material tested was:

Received from *Smith #926* Unit No. _____. Date *9·15·4-1* Time *1420*

Returned to *Smith #926* Unit No. _____. Date *10·26·4-1* Time *0850*

REMARKS:

_____

_____

Z-436

TRANSCRIPT OF SUPPRESSION MOTION:
State v. Frone

J = Judge
P = Prosecutor
D = Defense Counsel
R = S. Rosten

J: Next case. B-58374. State v. Frone.

P: Susan Schwartz for the State, Your Honor.

D: Noah Breen for defendant Frone, your honor. Mr. Frone is in court next to me. Your honor, we're here today for a motion to suppress. There's one live witness, Mr. Seth Rosten. Because the government carries the burden to justify a warrantless search, it is my understanding that Ms. Schwartz will be putting the witness on the stand, I'll cross-examine, then we'll argue.

J: It's your motion, counsel. If that's how you and the prosecutor want to do it, it's fine with me. Proceed.

D: Thank you, your honor.

P: We've also stipulated that if called to testify, Officer Smith would testify consistent with his police report, and that the report will be part of the record for this motion. I'd like the report marked State's #1 and moved into evidence.

J: Is that your understanding, counsel?

D: Yes, your honor.

J: Very well, the police report will be part of the record. Call your witness, Ms. Schwartz.

P: Thank you, your honor. The State calls Mr. Seth Rosten to the stand.

J: Mr. Rosten, please take the stand.

[Whereupon witness takes stand.]

J: Do you swear to tell the truth, the whole truth, and nothing but the truth?

R: I do.

J: Good. State your full name for the record, spelling your last name.

APPENDIX K

R: Seth Rosten. R-O-S-T-E-N.

J: Proceed, counsel.

P: Thank you, your honor. Mr. Rosten, where do you live?

R: 12203 Northpoint Drive, Nettletown.

P: And where are you employed?

R: Day 'N' Night Security Services.

P: How long have you been employed by Day 'N' Night?

R: 7 years.

P: What is Day 'N' Night?

R: It's a private security service. We contract out to guard all kinds of places …
       factories, schools, the airport.

P: Do you have any particular location you work?

R: Yes. The Nettletown Airport for the past 5 years.

P: Were you working at the airport on 9/9/Y-1?

R: Yes.

P: Focusing your attention on that day, do you recall where you were?

R: Yes.

P: Where were you?

R: I was working in the Eastwinds Airlines terminal, near the Skylift Lounge.

P: Did anything unusual happen?

R: Yes.

P: What was that?

R: I got a call over my radio from Nettletown Police Officer Dobbins.

P: What were the contents of the call?

D: Objection, hearsay.

P: Goes to probable cause.

J: Overruled. You may answer.

R: He said to be on the lookout for an adult white male, medium height, 5'9", about 170 pounds, brown overcoat, carrying blue garment bag with red stripe.

P: Did he say why you should be on the lookout for this man?

R: Yes.

P: Why?

R: He'd been dropped off at Eastwinds "Departures" about 10 minutes before by a man believed to be intoxicated on narcotics.

P: Did Officer Dobbins give you any instructions other than to be on the lookout?

R: Yes. He said to stop, identify and question the suspect because the Officer thought he might be involved in drug trafficking.

P: What did you do next?

R: I proceeded to walk through the ticketing area.

P: Did you see anyone fitting the description?

R: No.

P: What did you do next?

R: I checked Eastwinds' departure schedule to see when their next flight was.

P: Why did you do that?

R: I knew the guy'd been dropped off at Departures and I figured he might be catching a flight soon.

P: What did you find when you checked the schedule?

R: Eastwinds' next flight was at 4:15 p.m. to Los Angeles, Gate 11.

P: What did you do?

R: I went to the Gate 11 boarding area.

P: What happened next?

R: I saw a man coming out of the bathroom who fit the description I got from Officer Dobbins.

P: When you say fit the description, what do you mean?

R: Adult white male, mid-thirties, about 170 pounds, brown overcoat carrying blue garment bag. Medium height. Garment bag had red stripes.

P: Did you see that man in court today?

R: Yes.

P: Could you point him out and describe what he's wearing?

R: It's that guy next to the lawyer, wearing a plaid sports coat and red tie.

P: May the record reflect that Mr. Rosten has identified the defendant.

P: After seeing the defendant, what did you do then?

R: I walked up to Mr. Frone and asked if I might speak with him.

P: Did you have a weapon?

R: No.

P: Did you touch him?

R: At that time, no.

P: Do you recall your exact words?

R: Something like, "Sir, may I speak with you a moment?"

P: How did Mr. Frone reply?

R: He didn't say anything, just stopped next to me.

P: What happened next?

R: I asked for identification and he gave me his driver's license.

P: And then?

R: I called the Nettletown Police on my radio to tell them I'd made contact with the suspect but received no reply.

P: What happened next?

R: I decided to check his license against his ticket. You know, drug dealers often travel under phony names.

P: And did you do that?

R: Yes. I asked for his ticket. It was for the 4:15 flight to L.A. and matched his license.

P: What did you do with the license and ticket then?

R: Well, it all matched, so I gave the license and ticket back to him.

P: What happened then?

R: I still hadn't gotten a call back from the Nettletown Police and didn't know what they'd found since the first communication, so I asked Mr. Frone to accompany me to the Security Office.

P: The Security Office?

R: Yeah. It's just a little room with a desk, few chairs, a phone, and a computer.

P: Why did you want Mr. Frone to come to the Security Office?

R: I still hadn't heard from the police and wanted to wait at least a few more minutes to try to find out if they had any new information about possible drug trafficking before I let Frone go. I knew when his flight was leaving and I wasn't going to let him miss his flight if I hadn't heard from the police.

P: But why go to the Security Room?

R: Oh, yeah. We'd been standing right in the middle of the airport. People were watching, people who'd be on his flight. I thought that it must be getting embarrassing for Frone, and that we were beginning to cause a distraction in the airport.

P: How far was the Security Office from where you were standing?

R: 10' to 15'. Right across from the women's washroom.

P: What did Mr. Frone say when you asked him to accompany you to the Security Office?

R: He agreed.

P: Did you physically touch him or even threaten to touch him in any way?

R: Absolutely not.

P: What happened next?

R: We went to the Security Office and I ran his license number on our computer.

P: Why?

R: Just being careful. Never know if there're warrants. Also, I was still waiting to hear from the police and killing a little time.

P: What happened next?

R: I started to get uneasy.

P: What do you mean?

R: Well, we were in this small room. My back was partially to him when I worked the computer and I didn't have any weapon. And if he was involved in drugs, he might have a weapon and might be getting desperate.

P: What, if anything, did you do?

R: Well, I told him I wanted to frisk him.

P: Did he say anything?

R: Yes. At that moment, they announced his flight was going to start boarding in three minutes. He said he'd been cooperative and indicated he didn't want to miss his flight.

P: What did you do?

R: I asked him if he had anything to hide and he indicated he didn't, so I proceeded to pat-search him.

P: What happened next?

R: Inside his right jacket pocket I felt a flat solid object approximately 2" x 4".

P: What did you do then?

R: I reached in and removed it.

P: Why?

R: It could have been a weapon ... You know, a knife or razor in some little box, or even a little .25-caliber automatic. It certainly didn't feel like the usual stuff you find in people's pockets—comb, wallet, sunglasses, cigarettes, checkbook, lighter, address book ... You know.

P: What happened then?

R: Well, the object was wrapped in paper, so I began to unwrap it.

P: Did you see anything when you unwrapped it?

R: Yes. The paper appeared to be a hand-drawn map of the "Big Tree" area, and the object was a cassette tape.

P: What did you do then?

R: Well, I started to give him back his stuff and let him catch his plane when three thin hand-rolled cigarettes, one partially smoked, fell out of the unwrapped part of the map.

P: What did you do?

R: I bent down and picked them up.

P: Did you notice anything unusual about them?

R: Yes. From my training and experience they were clearly marijuana cigarettes.

P: What did you do then?

R: I ordered the defendant to sit down in the Security Office and handcuffed him. I placed the cigarettes in a clear plastic baggie, sealed it with tape, and marked the tape "S.R./Frone/9/9/Y-1." I did the same thing with the cassette tape. I then radioed the police again.

P: What happened then?

R: This time I reached them. They came right over and took Frone, the baggie I'd sealed, the cassette tape, and the map.

P: May I approach the witness, your honor?

J: Yes.

P: Mr. Rosten. Showing you what's been marked as State's #1 and State's #2 for identification, do you recognize what they are?

R: Yes.

P: What are they?

R: State's #1 is the three marijuana cigarettes I took from Mr. Frone ... #2 is the cassette tape.

P: How do you know that?

R: There's my baggie with my tape, initials and markings on each exhibit.

P: Are they different in any way from their condition when you gave them to the police?

R: Yes.

P: How?

R: They've got an outer bag and other seals and initials. Also, the cigarettes appear to have been cut open.

P: Other than that, are there any other differences?

R: No.

P: Thank you. No other questions at this time.

J: Cross-examine, counsel?

D: Yes, your honor. Thank you.

D: Mr. Rosten. Your company contracts with the State to provide security services to the airport?

R: Yes.

D: And before your company got that contract, the airport used to be watched over by Nettletown Police, correct?

R: That's my understanding.

D: OK, Mr. Rosten. Let's talk about that first call from the police and your initial contact with my client ...

D: Now, when you got that radio call, it told you what the driver was suspected of, didn't it?

R: Yes.

D: But you were not told to stop the driver, but the passenger, isn't that correct?

R: Yes.

D: The radio call told you "to stop, identify and question the suspect as he may be involved in drug traffic." Isn't that correct?

R: Yes.

D: The radio call didn't tell you that the passenger had been seen or known to be carrying drugs, did it?

R?   No.

D: The call didn't tell you that passenger was observed to be under influence of drugs either?

R: No.

D: The call said that the person under the influence was the driver, not the passenger, correct?

R: Yes.

D: And your walkie talkie call didn't say that anyone had seen the passenger commit any crimes at all?

R: No. It didn't.

D: In fact you didn't ask any questions of the person making the walkie talkie call at all, did you?

R: Not really.

D: And you didn't request any further information from that person, isn't that right?

R: Not at that time.

D: Now, when you saw the person who you thought was the passenger referred to in the radio call—you didn't call back and get further information before you stopped him?

R: No.

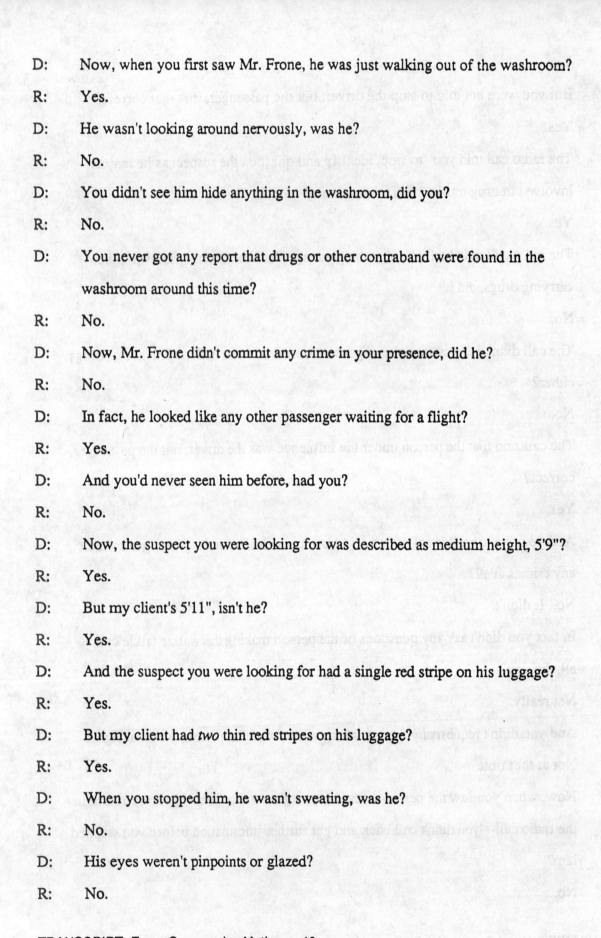

D: Now, when you first saw Mr. Frone, he was just walking out of the washroom?

R: Yes.

D: He wasn't looking around nervously, was he?

R: No.

D: You didn't see him hide anything in the washroom, did you?

R: No.

D: You never got any report that drugs or other contraband were found in the washroom around this time?

R: No.

D: Now, Mr. Frone didn't commit any crime in your presence, did he?

R: No.

D: In fact, he looked like any other passenger waiting for a flight?

R: Yes.

D: And you'd never seen him before, had you?

R: No.

D: Now, the suspect you were looking for was described as medium height, 5'9"?

R: Yes.

D: But my client's 5'11", isn't he?

R: Yes.

D: And the suspect you were looking for had a single red stripe on his luggage?

R: Yes.

D: But my client had *two* thin red stripes on his luggage?

R: Yes.

D: When you stopped him, he wasn't sweating, was he?

R: No.

D: His eyes weren't pinpoints or glazed?

R: No.

D: His speech wasn't slurred?

R: No.

D: He didn't try to run away or otherwise physically extricate himself from you?

R: No.

D: Now, the first thing you asked him to do was identify himself, correct?

R: Yes.

D: And he was able to identify himself properly?

R: Yes, I guess so.

D: He gave you his driver's license?

R: Yes.

D: And there wasn't anything at all wrong or even suspicious about his identification?

R: No. Not really.

D: Now, by then you knew that my client's name was Miller Frone, didn't you?

R: Yes.

D: You weren't familiar with that name, were you?

R: No.

D: Then you asked him where he was going and asked him to show his ticket to you?

R: Yes.

D: Did your walkie talkie call tell you to ask this question and demand his airline ticket?

R: No.

D: Now at the time you demanded the ticket, had you gotten any new information at all, since the radio call, that indicated my client was involved in criminal activity of any kind?

R: No.

D: Would it be fair to say, it was your decision to ask the question about destination and demand the ticket?

R: Yes. As I said, drug dealers often fly under false names and I just wanted to be sure.

D: Now, Mr. Frone answered your question, and gave you his ticket?

R: Yes.

D: And where did Mr. Frone's ticket say he was going?

R: Los Angeles.

D: So his ticket confirmed what he told you?

R: Yes.

D: Would it be fair to say his answers to your questions were consistent with his papers?

R: Yes.

D: Mr. Rosten, you've been assigned to airport duty five years?

R: Yes.

D: Have you ever flown yourself?

R: Yes. Many times.

D: You are aware that a passenger needs a ticket or boarding pass to take an airplane?

R: Yes.

D: So you knew, when you took Mr. Frone's ticket, that as long as you held it, he could not depart on his scheduled flight?

R: I guess so.

D: Now, I'd like to discuss moving my client to the security room and the warrant check ...

D: Now the next thing you did was ask him to accompany you to the security room?

R: Yes.

D: You hadn't learned anything new, incriminating about Mr. Frone at this time?

R: No.

D: You didn't tell Mr. Frone he didn't have to go with you?

R: I asked him to come.

D: You didn't tell him that he didn't have to?

R: No.

D: You didn't tell him he was free to go?

R: No.

D: By the way, Mr. Rosten, were you wearing a security guard uniform?

R: Yes.

D: Could you describe it for us?

R: Blue hat, coat, and pants. With the Day 'N' Night logo on the sleeve.

D: Do you wear a badge?

R: Yes.

D: Mr. Frone followed you to the security office, didn't he?

R: Yes.

D: And once you got there, he sat in a chair while you ran his driver's license, didn't he?

R: Yes.

D: No one told you to take Mr. Frone to the security office or run his license?

R: No. It was my idea. Fairly routine procedure.

D: Nothing showed up on the computer, did it?

R: What do you mean?

D: You didn't find any warrants, did you?

R: No.

D: And all this time you were waiting for a call back from the police?

R: Yes.

D: Mr. Rosten, now let's talk about the frisk …

D: Now, Mr. Frone did everything you asked him to do, didn't he?

R: Yes.

D: Did he ever threaten you in any way?

R: No.

D: In fact, he cooperated with each request?

R: Yes.

D: Yet you decided to pat him down "for weapons," I believe you said on direct?

R: Yes. It was a small room and possible drugs were involved.

D: Now, your initial information from airport police didn't mention any weapons, did it?

R: No, not weapons, specifically. But again, we were dealing with possible drugs, and weapons come with the territory.

D: And you didn't pat-search Mr. Frone when you first detained him?

R: No.

D: You didn't pat him when you first transported him to the security room?

R: No.

D: You didn't pat him when you first entered the security room?

R: No.

D: In fact, you didn't pat him when, for over 5 minutes, you sat with your back to him, running his name on the computer?

R: I don't know if it was 5 minutes.

D: Now, nothing happened between the time you *first* stopped Mr. Frone and the time, almost 10 minutes later, you frisked him, did it?

R: What do you mean, "nothing?"

D: Mr. Frone never threatened you and you received no more information from the police?

R: No.

D: When you say pat search for weapons, that would mean guns and knives and the like, wouldn't it?

R: Yes.

D: Are you aware of any guns that do not have metal barrels, chambers and magazines?

R: No. I am not. But I'm not a firearms expert.

D: Now, it is not forbidden to carry all knives on an airliner, is it?

R: No. There are some you can take, if they're small enough.

D: In fact, one may carry a pocketknife, if it has a small enough blade, isn't that true?

R: Yes.

D: But a passenger cannot carry a fixed blade knife, true?

R: True.

D: Are you aware of any pocketknives that have blades of any other material than metal?

R: No.

D: Now, there is a metal detector through which all departing passengers must pass, isn't that correct?

R: Yes.

D: And that metal detector is at the entrance to the boarding gates, isn't it?

R: Yes.

D: So Mr. Frone would have already passed through that machine by the time you contacted, detained and frisked him, isn't that correct?

R: Yes.

D: If Mr. Frone had possessed a gun or knife or other weapon of metal that set off the metal detector, it would have been removed from him, as far as you know, isn't that correct?

R: I guess so.

D: You knew this at the time you stopped Mr. Frone, isn't that true?

R: Yes.

D: Let's talk about removing the object . . .

D: Now, when you patted on the outside of Mr. Frone's clothing, you felt a flat solid object about 2" x 4", isn't that correct?

R: Yes.

D: It felt rectangular, didn't it?

R: Yes.

D: Would it be fair to say it felt like small box?

R: Could have been.

D: Mr. Rosten, you have never seen a 2" x 4" flat rectangular box that was a gun?

R: Possibly a .25-caliber automatic could be around that size.

D: But it's not a *box*, is it?

R: No.

D: And you've never seen such a knife?

R: No. But a knife could fit in a box.

D: Now, you didn't feel any tube or barrel, did you?

R: No.

D: You didn't feel a handle, did you?

R: No.

D: And you had no specific information that any weapons were involved in this situation?

R: Not any specific information, other than drugs might be involved.

D: Now, Mr. Frone did not try to pull away or push your hand away when you went to frisk him, did he?

R: No.

D: And he never made any move, sudden or otherwise, towards his pockets?

R: No.

D: No further questions, your honor.

J: Any re-direct for the government?

P: No, your honor.

J: May this witness then be excused?

P: Yes.

D: Yes.

J: All right. I'll hear argument. Defense counsel, it's your motion.

CREDIT CARD IMPRINT   ORIGINAL   9/8/Y-1

3931 399641 81009 09/Y+2	RETURN LOCATION	RENTAL AGREEMENT

CREDIT CARD/DIRECT BILL NO./PO.NO./EXP.DATE

	REPLACEMENT			ORIGINAL	
ARRIVAL DATE/METHOD/TIME/MP/CAR TYPE/C.A. OR U/RETURN DATE	COMM.	PERSONAL	OWNING LOC.	VEHICLE NO.		CLASS

RENTER GILBERT J. JARDINE   LL3-617   LICENSE NO.

PHONE NO./D.O.B./RAPID ACTION NO. (001) 644-4174   MAKE MODEL CAMERO Y-10   MAX PAYLOAD

RESIDENCE 2157 Cherry Ave   MLS IN   TIME IN

CITY/STATE/ZIP NETTLETOWN, OOO71   MLS OUT (UNLIMITED) TIME OUT

LICENSE NO./EXP. DATE/STATE GJJ 561 PX   MLS DRVN   RENTAL TIME   RENTAL TIME

COMPANY "GRO GREEN"   MIN/MAX RENTAL

COMPANY PHONE NO./CORPORATE RATE NO. SAME

LOCAL CONTACT/PHONE NO.   MILEAGE ALLOWANCE

ADDITIONAL DRIVER/D.O.B.

LICENSE NO./EXP. DATE/STATE   PREPAID VOUCHER OR COUPON VALUE

REMARK   **ATTENTION**
DAILY RATE IS BASED ON 24 HOUR DAY MINIMUM CHARGE DISCOUNT RATES ONLY FOR SPECIFIED PERIOD RATES DO NOT INCLUDE REFUELING SERVICE CHARGE   TOTAL TIME/MILEAGE   DISCOUNT TOTAL —

UNLIMITED MILEAGE, WEEKEND SPECIAL AND VACATION SPECIAL RATES DO NOT APPLY IF VEHICLE IS RETURNED TO A LOCATION OTHER THAN THE RENTING LOCATION. DISCOUNT RATES ONLY FOR SPECIFIED PERIOD.   [ ] RENTER AGREES TO FUEL PURCHASE OPTION (SEE PARA. 12B ON REVERSE SIDE)   RETURN LOCATION CHARGE

I AGREE TO RETURN THIS VEHICLE ON OR BEFORE THE INDICATED DUE BACK DATE TO THE SAME LOCATION AT WHICH IT WAS RENTED OR TO THE BUDGET OFFICE SPECIFIED IN THE BOX BELOW A DROP CHARGE MAY APPLY IF VEHICLE RETURNED TO OTHER THAN RENTING LOCATION

DUE BACK 9.15.Y-1   AUTHORIZED RETURN   RENTER'S INIT x GJJ

LOSS DAMAGE WAIVER (LDW) -- Renter initials below to accept or decline the optional LDW at the rate shown for each day or fraction thereof. If Renter declines LDW, renter will be responsible for the FULL VALUE (program vehicles values are set by the manufacturer and will be higher than market value) of any loss of a damage to the vehicle, regardless of fault. IN PARAGRAPH 8 LDW NOT INSURANCE RENTER'S OWN VEHICLE INSURANCE MAY COVER ALL OR PART OF SUCH LOSS OR DAMAGE RENTER MAY WANT TO VERIFY BEFORE ACCEPTING LDW.

X _____   x GJJ
ACCEPTS   DECLINES

PERSONAL ACCIDENTAL INSURANCE (P.A.K.)
RENTER INITIALS TO ACCEPT AT RATE SHOWN, OR DECLINE. PAI FOR RENTER AND HIS IMMEDIATE FAMILY, IF "ACCEPTS" RENTER ACKNOWLEDGES TO HAVE READ, AND UNDERSTANDS THE BROCHURE GIVEN TO HIM AT THE TIME OF RENTAL WHICH DESCRIBES THE COVERAGE AND LIMITS.

X _____   x GJJ

PERSONAL EFFECTS COVERAGE (P.E.C.)
IF OFFERED, RENTER INITIALS TO ACCEPT AT RATE SHOWN OR DECLINE P.E.C. FOR COVERAGE OF PERSONAL PROPERTY OF RENTER AND HIS IMMEDIATE FAMILY. IF "ACCEPTS" RENTER ACKNOWLEDGES TO HAVE READ, AND UNDERSTANDS THE BROCHURE GIVEN TO HIM AT THE TIME OF RENTAL WHICH DESCRIBES THE COVERAGE AND LIMITS.   IF RENTER RETURNS THE VEHICLE WITH LESS FUEL THAN WHEN RENTED A REFUELING CHARGE WILL APPLY.

X _____   x GJJ

CARGO INSURANCE CE
BY INITIALING, CUSTOMER ACCEPTS AT RATE SHOWN, OR DECLINES CARGO INSURANCE CUSTOMER REPRESENTS TO HAVE READ AND UNDERSTANDS BROCHURE MADE AVAILABLE AT THE TIME OF RENTAL DESCRIBING COVERAGE AND LIMITS.   RENTAL AGREEMENT NO.   SUB TOTAL 117 24

X _____   x GJJ

II HAVE READ UNDERSTAND AND AGREE TO BE BOUND BY THE TERMS AND CONDITIONS ON BOTH SIDES OF THIS AGREEMENT, ESPECIALLY THE ldw SECTION SET FORTH ABOVE, IF THIS RENTAL IS TO BE CHARGED ON A CREDIT CARD, MY SIGNATURE BELOW WILL BE CONSIDERED TO HAVE BEEN MADE ON THE APPLICABLE CREDIT CARD VOUCHER AND I GIVE BUDGET PERMISSION TO FILL OUT AND SIGN THE VOUCHER.   BILLING TYPE/AMOUNT   LESS DEPOSIT
                                                                           NET DUE RENTER   NET DUE 117 24

x G.J.Jardine
RENTERS SIGNATURE   NETTLECARD

PREPARED BY   CLOSED BY   CONTRACT CLOSED SUBJECT TO FINAL AUDIT

APPENDIX L-1

Nettle Car & Truck Rental ▬▬▬

CREDIT CARD IMPRINT	ORIGINAL					9/8/Y-1	
3931 399641 81009 09/Y+2	RETURN LOCATION					RENTAL AGREEMENT	

CREDIT CARD/DIRECT BILL NO./PO.NO/EXP.DATE	REPLACEMENT				ORIGINAL	
	COMM.	PERSONAL	OWNING LOC.			
ARRIVAL DATE/METHOD/TIME/MP/CAR TYPE/C.A. OR U/RETURN DATE			VEHICLE NO.			CLASS
RENTER GILBERT J. JARDINE LL3-209			LICENSE NO.			
PHONE NO./D.O.B./RAPID ACTION NO. (001) 644-4174 COUGAR Y-10			MAKE MODEL	MAX PAYLOAD		
RESIDENCE 2157 CHERRY AVE.	MLS IN		TIME IN			
CITY/STATE/ZIP NETTLETOWN 00071	MLS OUT (UNLIMITED)		TIME OUT			
LICENSE NO./EXP. DATE/STATE GJ 561 PX	MLS DRVN	RENTAL TIME		RENTAL TIME		
COMPANY "OND-GREEN"	MIN/MAX RENTAL					
COMPANY PHONE NO./CORPORATE RATE NO. SAME						
LOCAL CONTACT/PHONE NO.	MILEAGE ALLOWANCE					
ADDITIONAL DRIVER/D.O.B.						
LICENSE NO./EXP. DATE/STATE	PREPAID VOUCHER OR COUPON VALUE					
REMARK	ATTENTION DAILY RATE IS BASED ON 24 HOUR DAY MINIMUM CHARGE DISCOUNT RATES ONLY FOR SPECIFIED PERIOD RATES DO NOT INCLUDE REFUELING SERVICE CHARGE			TOTAL TIME/ MILEAGE		
				DISCOUNT TOTAL		

UNLIMITED MILEAGE, WEEKEND SPECIAL AND VACATION SPECIAL RATES DO NOT APPLY IF VEHICLE IS RETURNED TO A LOCATION OTHER THAN THE RENTING LOCATION. DISCOUNT RATES ONLY FOR SPECIFIED PERIOD.

[ ] RENTER AGREES TO FUEL PURCHASE OPTION (SEE PARA. 12B ON REVERSE SIDE)

RETURN LOCATION CHARGE

I AGREE TO RETURN THIS VEHICLE ON OR BEFORE THE INDICATED DUE BACK DATE TO THE SAME LOCATION AT WHICH IT WAS RENTED OR TO THE BUDGET OFFICE SPECIFIED IN THE BOX BELOW A DROP CHARGE MAY APPLY IF VEHICLE RETURNED TO OTHER THAN RENTING LOCATION

DUE BACK 9.15. Y-1	AUTHORIZED RETURN	RENTER'S INIT X GJJ

LOSS DAMAGE WAIVER (LDW) -- Renter initials below to accept or decline the optional LDW at the rate shown for each day or fraction thereof. If Renter declines LDW, renter will be responsible for the FULL VALUE (program vehicles value are set by the manufacturer and will be higher than market value) of any loss of a damage to the vehicle, regardless of fault. IN PARAGRAPH 8 LDW NOT INSURANCE RENTER'S OWN VEHICLE INSURANCE MAY COVER ALL OR PART OF SUCH LOSS OR DAMAGE RENTER MAY WANT TO VERIFY BEFORE ACCEPTING LDW.

X _____ ACCEPTS   X GJJ DECLINES

PERSONAL ACCIDENTAL INSURANCE (P.A.K.) RENTER INITIALS TO ACCEPT AT RATE SHOWN, OR DECLINE. PAI FOR RENTER AND HIS IMMEDIATE FAMILY. IF "ACCEPTS" RENTER ACKNOWLEDGES TO HAVE READ, AND UNDERSTANDS THE BROCHURE GIVEN TO HIM AT THE TIME OF RENTAL WHICH DESCRIBES THE COVERAGE AND LIMITS.

X _____   X GJJ

PERSONAL EFFECTS COVERAGE (P.E.C) IF OFFERED, RENTER INITIALS TO ACCEPT AT RATE SHOWN OR DECLINE P.E.C. FOR COVERAGE OF PERSONAL PROPERTY OF RENTER AND HIS IMMEDIATE FAMILY. IF "ACCEPTS" RENTER ACKNOWLEDGES TO HAVE READ, AND UNDERSTANDS THE BROCHURE GIVEN TO HIM AT THE TIME OF RENTAL WHICH DESCRIBES THE COVERAGE AND LIMITS.

X _____   X GJJ

IF RENTER RETURNS THE VEHICLE WITH LESS FUEL THAN WHEN RENTED A REFUELING CHARGE WILL APPLY.

CARGO INSURANCE CE BY INITIALING, CUSTOMER ACCEPTS AT RATE SHOWN, OR DECLINES CARGO INSURANCE CUSTOMER REPRESENTS TO HAVE READ AND UNDERSTANDS BROCHURE MADE AVAILABLE AT THE TIME OF RENTAL DESCRIBING COVERAGE AND LIMITS.

X GJJ

RENTAL AGREEMENT NO.	SUB-TOTAL	117.24

II HAVE READ UNDERSTAND AND AGREE TO BE BOUND BY THE TERMS AND CONDITIONS ON BOTH SIDES OF THIS AGREEMENT, ESPECIALLY THE ldw SECTION SET FORTH ABOVE. IF THIS RENTAL IS TO BE CHARGED ON A CREDIT CARD, MY SIGNATURE BELOW WILL BE CONSIDERED TO HAVE BEEN MADE ON THE APPLICABLE CREDIT CARD VOUCHER AND I GIVE BUDGET PERMISSION TO FILL OUT AND SIGN THE VOUCHER.

X G. J. Jardine
RENTERS SIGNATURE

BILLING TYPE/AMOUNT NETTLE CARD	LESS DEPOSIT		
		NET DUE RENTER	NET DUE 117.24

PREPARED BY	CLOSED BY	CONTRACT CLOSED SUBJECT TO FINAL AUDIT

APPENDIX L-2

```
┌─────────────────────────────────────────────┬──────────────┬──────────────┐
│  3931 399641 81009                            │ CARDMEMBER   │ EXPIRATION   │
│  Cardmember Account Number                    │ USE  [ ]     │ DATE [✓]     │
│                                               │              │ CHECKED      │
├───────────────────────────────────────────────┬─────────────────────────────┤
│  09/Y-1 THRU 09/Y-2                            │ Approval Code  │Type of Delayed Chg.│
│                                                ├────────────────┼───────────────────┤
│  GILBERT J. JARDINE                            │ Number or Bill No. │Amt. Of Delayed Chg.│
│                                                │         I      │     I             │
├───────────────────────────────────────────────┼─────────────────────────────┤
│ Service Establishment    Date of Charge  (DEPOSIT)  │    Revised Total         │
│                                    CAMERO LL3-617   │  COUGAR L43-29           │
│              09 08 Y-1                              │                          │
│  AJAX RENTAL WRECKS                 MERCHANDISE/SERVICES                       │
│  137 MAIN STREET.                   [N][ ][ ][ ] [ ][ ]                        │
│  NETTLETOWN, _____00074            TAXES                                      │
│                                     [ ][ ][N][ ] [ ][ ]                        │
│                                     TIPS/MISC.                                 │
│              PLEASE PRINT FIRMLY     [ ][ ][ ][N] [ ][ ]                       │
├───────────────────────────────────────────────────────────────────────────┤
│ Cardmember Signature                 Total                                    │
│  X  G. J. Jardine                    [ ][ ][ ][ ] [ ][ ]                      │
├───────────────────────────────────────────────────────────────────────────┤
│ Merchandise and/or service purchased on this card    │  DOLLARS   │  CENTS    │
│ shall not be resold or returned for cash refund.     │            │           │
│ Establishment agrees to transmit to American Express │            │           │
│ Travel Related Services Co., Inc. Or authorized      │            │           │
│ representative for payment.                           │            │           │
├──────────────┬──────────────────────────────────────┴────────────┴───────────┤
│ BANK OF      │  NETTLE                                                         │
│ NETTLETOWN   │  Card          707403          Cardmember Copy                  │
│              │              Invoice Number                                     │
└──────────────┴─────────────────────────────────────────────────────────────┘
```

APPENDIX M

APPENDIX N

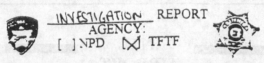

INVESTIGATION REPORT
AGENCY:
[ ] NPD [X] TFTF

Page 1 of 2

1 Public Disclosure Act	OTHER: _____

2 Arrest	3 Vehicle	4 Juvenile	8 Report Name/Offense
5 Property	6 Medical	7 Domestic Viol	TAPE FRAUD INVESTIGATION

9 Type of Premise (For vehicles, state where parked.)	10 Entry Point	11 Method

12 Weapon /Tool/Force Used	13 Date Reported 9.28.Y-1	14 Time Reported	15 Date Occurrence	16 Time Occurrence	17 Day of Week

18 Location of: Incident [ ] Address [ ]		19 Census	20 Dist.

PERSONS/BUSINESS INVOLVED

CODE   C (Person Reporting Complaint)   V (Victim)   W (Witness)   P (Parent)   VB (Victim Business)   O (Other)

21 Code	22 NAME: Last	First	Middle (Maiden)	23 Race/Sex	24 Date of Birth	25 Home Phone
26 DPA	27 ADDRESS: Street	City	State	Zip	28 Place of Employment/School	29 Business Phone
21 Code	22 NAME: Last	First	Middle (Maiden)	23 Race/Sex	24 Date of Birth	25 Home Phone
26 DPA	27 ADDRESS: Street	City	State	Zip	28 Place of Employment/School	29 Business Phone
21 Code	22 NAME: Last	First	Middle (Maiden)	23 Race/Sex	24 Date of Birth	25 Home Phone
26 DPA	27 ADDRESS: Street	City	State	Zip	28 Place of Employment/School	29 Business Phone

[ ] Additional persons on Report Continuation Sheet (People) Form No. Z-556

CODE: A (Arrest)   S (Suspect)   SV (Suspect Verified)   R (Runaway)   M (Missing Person)   I (Institutional Impact)

PERSON NUMBER 1

30 Code	31 NAME: Last	First	Middle (Maiden)	32 Home Phone	33 Business Phone
S	JARDINE	GILBERT	J		

34 ADDRESS: Street	City	State	Zip	35 Occupation	36 Place of Employment/School	37 Relation to Victim
2157 CHERRY AVE.	NETTLETOWN		00071			

38 Date of Birth	39 Race	40 Sex	41 Height	42 Weight/Build	43 Hair	44 Eyes	45 Clothing, Scars, marks, Tattoos, Peculiarities, A.K.A.

46 Number [ ] Booked [ ] Cited	47 Charge Details (Include Ordinance or R.C.W. Number)

PERSON NUMBER 2

30 Code	31 NAME: Last	First	Middle (Maiden)	32 Home Phone	33 Business Phone

34 ADDRESS: Street	City	State	Zip	35 Occupation	36 Place of Employment/School	37 Relation to Victim

38 Date of Birth	39 Race	40 Sex	41 Height	42 Weight/Build	43 Hair	44 Eyes	45 Clothing, Scars, marks, Tattoos, Peculiarities, A.K.A.

46 Number [ ] Booked [ ] Cited	47 Charge Details (Include Ordinance or R.C.W. Number)

[ ] Additional persons on Report Continuation Sheet (People) Form No. Z-556   Juvenile Arrests - Block No. 109 MUST Be completed

VEHICLE

48 Stolen	49 Victim	50 Impound	54 License No.	55 Lic/State	56 Lic/Year	57 Lic/Type	58 Vin.
51 Recovery	52 Suspect	53 Hold					

59 Year	60 Make	61 Model	62 Body Style	63 Color	64 Peculiarities	65 Hold Requested by/For

66 Ori. & Case No.	67 Registered Owner: Name	Address	City	State	Zip	68 Home Phone

69 Condition [ ] Drivable [ ] Not Drivable [ ] Stripped [ ] Wrecked	70 Inventory

70 Inventory (Continued)   71 Tow Co. & Signature

72 Enter	73 Date	74 Time	75 WACIC	76 LESA	77 Initial	78 Release Info	79 Date	80 Time	81 Release No.	82 Releasing Authority
83 Clear	84	85	86	87	88	89 Owner Notified	90	91	92 Operator's Name	

93 Signature & I.D. No. of Reporting Officer(s) A. Morris (#301)	94 Approval	95 Distribution Excp.

REPORT PROCESSING (Records Personnel Only)	DISTRIBUTION: DATE ____ BY ____ INDEXED: DATE ____ BY ____	Microfilmed Initials____	Filed Initials____

C3:\C\P\JPOLICE.RPT

APPENDIX O

NARRATIVE:

On 09/18/Y-1, received referral of investigation from Officer Smith of Nettletown Police Department. Officer Smith provided us with two cassettes taken from individuals at the Nettletown Airport, a hand-drawn map of the "Big Tree" area, various documents seized from a Y-10 Camaro, and two boxes of cassette tapes found in a search of a Y-10 Cougar.

On 09/28/Y-1, I delivered all tapes to Dr. Sally Sands, acoustical fraud expert for the TFTF, for inspection. After examining the tapes, Dr. Sands determined that they were high-quality bootleg tapes of live concerts throughout the state over the past year.

SUPPLEMENTAL REPORT

Crime: Possible Tape Fraud	Case No.: Investig.	CB: 436	District: 46
Victim: Unknown		Addr:	

_____**Narrative**_____

    Carton containing nearly 2,000 cassette tapes were presented to TFTT expert technician S. Sand on 9/28/Y-1, for inspection. Random testing of tapes confirmed that unauthorized copies of various live concerts.

Page 1

Date: 9/30/Y-1	Technician: S. Sand #971		Approval
Distr. Date: _____	By: _____	Microfilmed: _____	By: _____
Indexed: _____	By: _____	Copy to: _____	

C2\C\\TPEFRAUD.FTF

APPENDIX P

LABORATORY REPORT

Crime: Possible Tape Fraud	Case No.:Investig.	CB: 436	District: 46
Victim: Unknown		Addr:	

Date of Lab Work: 9/30/Y-1

Examination Requested: PROCESS FOR POSSIBLE UNAUTHORIZED COPYING.

Requested by: TFTF

_____ **Details** _____

Items Processed: ITEM #-1 2,000 (approx.) cassette tapes.

Evidence Obtained: **At Scene [ ]   Other Officer [ ]   Property Room [X]**

Results/Remarks:

ITEM #1, 2,000 cassette tapes (approx) were randomly inspected for possible unauthorized copying. The results of this search is positive for unauthorized duplication of various live concerts.

Page 1

Date: 10/3/Y-1	Technician: S. Sand #971			Approval
Distr. Date: _____	By: _____	Microfilmed: _____	By: _____	
Indexed: _____	By: _____	Copy to: _____		

C2\C\J\TPEFRAUD.LAB

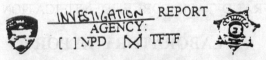

1	Public Disclosure Act		OTHER: _____		

2 Arrest	3 Vehicle	4 Juvenile	8 Report Name/Offense
5 Property	6 Medical	7 Domestic Viol	TAPE FRAUD INVESTIGATION

9 Type of Premise (For vehicles, state where parked.)	10 Entry Point	11 Method

12 Weapon /Tool/Force Used	13 Date Reported	14 Time Reported	15 Date Occurrence	16 Time Occurrence	17 Day of Week
	10.13.Y-1	1237	10.13.Y-1	1237	

18 Location of: Incident [ ] Address [ ]					19 Census	20 Dist.

PERSONS/BUSINESS INVOLVED

CODE	C (Person Reporting Complaint)	V (Victim)	W (Witness)	P (Parent)	VB (Victim Business)	O (Other)		
21 Code	22 NAME: Last	First	Middle (Maiden)		23 Race/Sex	24 Date of Birth		25 Home Phone
26 DPA	27 ADDRESS: Street	City	State	Zip	28 Place of Employment/School			29 Business Phone
21 Code	22 NAME: Last	First	Middle (Maiden)		23 Race/Sex	24 Date of Birth		25 Home Phone
26 DPA	27 ADDRESS: Street	City	State	Zip	28 Place of Employment/School			29 Business Phone
21 Code	22 NAME: Last	First	Middle (Maiden)		23 Race/Sex	24 Date of Birth		25 Home Phone
26 DPA	27 ADDRESS: Street	City	State	Zip	28 Place of Employment/School			29 Business Phone

[ ] Additional persons on Report Continuation Sheet (People) Form No. Z-556

CODE:	A (Arrest)	S (Suspect)	SV (Suspect Verified)	R (Runaway)	M (Missing Person)	I (Institutional Impact)

PERSON NUMBER 1

30 Code	31 NAME: Last	First	Middle (Maiden)			32 Home Phone	33 Business Phone
S	JARDINE	GILBERT	J				

34 ADDRESS: Street	City	State	Zip	35 Occupation	36 Place of Employment/School	37 Relation to Victim
2157 CHERRY AVE.	NETTLETOWN		00071			

38 Date of Birth	39 Race	40 Sex	41 Height	42 Weight/Build	43 Hair	44 Eyes	45 Clothing, Scars, marks, Tattoos, Peculiarities, A.K.A.

46 [ ] Booked [ ] Cited	Number	47 Charge Details (Include Ordinance or R.C.W. Number)

PERSON NUMBER 2

30 Code	31 NAME: Last	First	Middle (Maiden)			32 Home Phone	33 Business Phone

34 ADDRESS: Street	City	State	Zip	35 Occupation	36 Place of Employment/School	37 Relation to Victim

38 Date of Birth	39 Race	40 Sex	41 Height	42 Weight/Build	43 Hair	44 Eyes	45 Clothing, Scars, marks, Tattoos, Peculiarities, A.K.A.

46 [ ] Booked [ ] Cited	Number	47 Charge Details (Include Ordinance or R.C.W. Number)

[ ] Additional persons on Report Continuation Sheet (People) Form No. Z-556   Juvenile Arrests - Block No. 109 MUST Be completed

VEHICLE

48 Stolen	49 Victim	50 Impound	54 License No.	55 Lic/State	56 Lic/Year	57 Lic/Type	58 Vin.
51 Recovery	52 Suspect	53 Hold					

59 Year	60 Make	61 Model	62 Body Style	63 Color	64 Peculiarities	65 Hold Requested by/For	

66 Ori. & Case No.	67 Registered Owner: Name		Address	City	State	Zip	68 Home Phone

69 Condition [ ] Drivable [ ] Not Drivable [ ] Stripped [ ] Wrecked	70 Inventory	
70 Inventory (Continued)		71 Tow Co. & Signature

72 Enter	73 Date	74 Time	75 WACIC	76 LESA	77 Initial	78 Release Info	79 Date	80 Time	81 Release No.	82 Releasing Authority
83 Clear	84	85	86	87	88	89 Owner Notified	90	91	92 Operator's Name	

93 Signature & I.D. No. of Reporting Officer(s)	94 Approval	95 Distribution Excp.
A. Morris (#301)		

REPORT PROCESSING (Records Personnel Only)	DISTRIBUTION: DATE _____ BY _____ INDEXED: DATE _____ BY _____	Microfilmed Initials _____	Filed Initials _____

C3:\C\PA\POLICE.RPT

APPENDIX Q

NARRATIVE

On 10/6/Y-1, I received a call from Officer Dubow (Badge #642) of the Nettletown Police Department, who reported to me that a reliable informant had just told him that the bootleg tapes were being made at a place called "The Rancho." The informant didn't know where it was but said, "Gil runs the place." Also, information and moneys involved in the operation were being exchanged through P.O. Box #609 at the main Nettletown Post Office. Officer Dubow states that this confidential informant has provided information that led to the arrest and conviction of two drug traffickers in the Nettletown area.

Based on this information, and with the assistance of Postal Officials, TFTF officers wired Post Office Box #609 to connect with a light in a surveillance van so that it would be known to the occupants of the van when anyone opened the suspect box. At approximately 1440 hours on 10/13/Y-1, an unidentified male Caucasian, age 26, 160 lbs., 5'9", short brown hair wearing blue jeans and a Nettletown Tigers warm-up jacket was seen to take a package from the box after the light alerted TFTF officers.

Officers Henry Fellows and Jay Johnson followed the suspect as he headed north out of the downtown area. At the edge of the "Big Tree" area officers lost the Y-5 Pontiac Firebird, license number BUH 707. Later, back at headquarters, we discovered that the area in which the officers lost the suspect Firebird was consistent with the hand-drawn map found around the tape taken from Miller Frone on September 9. The license number was subsequently run and found registered to William Bean, Crestview Apts. #601, 521 Crestview Ave. Attempts to contact Bean proved unsuccessful.

| 1 | Public Disclosure Act | OTHER: _____ |

| 2 Arrest | 3 Vehicle | 4 Juvenile | 8 Report Name/Offense |
| 5 Property | 6 Medical | 7 Domestic Viol | TAPE FRAUD INVESTIGATION |

| 9 Type of Premise (For vehicles, state where parked.) | 10 Entry Point | 11 Method |

12 Weapon/Tool/Force Used	13 Date Reported	14 Time Reported	15 Date Occurrence	16 Time Occurrence	17 Day of Week
	10.30.Y-1 1700				
18 Location of: Incident [ ] Address [ ]	11.9.Y-1 1300		19 Census	20 Dist.

PERSONS/BUSINESS INVOLVED

CODE   C (Person Reporting Complaint)   V (Victim)   W (Witness)   P (Parent)   VB (Victim Business)   O (Other)

21 Code	22 NAME: Last	First	Middle (Maiden)	23 Race/Sex	24 Date of Birth	25 Home Phone
26 DPA	27 ADDRESS: Street	City	State	Zip	28 Place of Employment/School	29 Business Phone
21 Code	22 NAME: Last	First	Middle (Maiden)	23 Race/Sex	24 Date of Birth	25 Home Phone
26 DPA	27 ADDRESS: Street	City	State	Zip	28 Place of Employment/School	29 Business Phone
21 Code	22 NAME: Last	First	Middle (Maiden)	23 Race/Sex	24 Date of Birth	25 Home Phone
26 DPA	27 ADDRESS: Street	City	State	Zip	28 Place of Employment/School	29 Business Phone

[ ] Additional persons on Report Continuation Sheet (People) Form No. Z-556

PERSON NUMBER 1

CODE: A (Arrest)   S (Suspect)   SV (Suspect Verified)   R (Runaway)   M (Missing Person)   I (Institutional Impact)

30 Code	31 NAME: Last	First	Middle (Maiden)	32 Home Phone	33 Business Phone
S	JARDINE	GILBERT	J		
34 ADDRESS: Street	City	State	Zip	35 Occupation	36 Place of Employment/School	37 Relation to Victim
2157 CHERRY AVE. NETTLETOWN		00071			
38 Date of Birth	39 Race	40 Sex	41 Height	42 Weight/Build	43 Hair	44 Eyes	45 Clothing, Scars, marks, Tattoos, Peculiarities, A.K.A.
46 Number [ ] Booked [ ] Cited	47 Charge Details (Include Ordinance or R.C.W. Number)

PERSON NUMBER 2

30 Code	31 NAME: Last	First	Middle (Maiden)	32 Home Phone	33 Business Phone
34 ADDRESS: Street	City	State	Zip	35 Occupation	36 Place of Employment/School	37 Relation to Victim
38 Date of Birth	39 Race	40 Sex	41 Height	42 Weight/Build	43 Hair	44 Eyes	45 Clothing, Scars, marks, Tattoos, Peculiarities, A.K.A.
46 Number [ ] Booked [ ] Cited	47 Charge Details (Include Ordinance or R.C.W. Number)

[ ] Additional persons on Report Continuation Sheet (People) Form No. Z-556   Juvenile Arrests - Block No. 109 MUST Be completed

VEHICLE

48 Stolen	49 Victim	50 Impound	54 License No.	55 Lic/State	56 Lic/Year	57 Lic/Type	58 Vin.
51 Recovery	52 Suspect	53 Hold					
59 Year	60 Make	61 Model	62 Body Style	63 Color	64 Peculiarities	65 Hold Requested by/For	
66 Ori. & Case No.	67 Registered Owner: Name		Address	City	State	Zip	68 Home Phone

| 69 Condition [ ] Drivable [ ] Not Drivable [ ] Stripped [ ] Wrecked | 70 Inventory |
| 70 Inventory (Continued) | 71 Tow Co. & Signature |

| 72 Enter | 73 Date | 74 Time | 75 WACIC | 76 LESA | 77 Initial | 78 Release Info | 79 Date | 80 Time | 81 Release No. | 82 Releasing Authority |
| 83 Clear | 84 | 85 | 86 | 87 | 88 | 89 Owner Notified | 90 | 91 | 92 Operator's Name | |

| 93 Signature & I.D. No. of Reporting Officer(s) | 94 Approval | 95 Distribution Excp. |
| A. Morris (#301) | | |

| REPORT PROCESSING (Records Personnel Only) | DISTRIBUTION: DATE _____ BY _____ INDEXED: DATE _____ BY _____ | Microfilmed Initials_____ | Filed Initials_____ |

C3:\C\P\\POLICE.RPT

APPENDIX R

NARRATIVE

On my orders, a helicopter flew surveillance over the "Big Tree" area. Equipped with listening devices and infrared detection equipment, TFTF officers located a possible location for the manufacture of bootleg tapes. Even with their equipment, officers were barely able to make out what appeared to be a large central structure with several outbuildings. This difficulty was due in part to the fact that the buildings were located in a thickly wooded area and and in part that they appeared to be painted "camouflage style." Under the circumstances, I thought it appropriate to seek help from the military in the form of satellite surveillance. I contacted Lt. Col. Winters at Lepin Field and received his approval. Photographs from the satellite clearly showed a large main house and four outbuildings, several trucks being loaded with boxes similar in size to the ones found in the Cougar, and numerous people working around the main building. Based on this information, I decided to attempt to send an undercover officer into the location.

Early the next day, a TFTF officer, Dale Snopt, entered the suspect property disguised in Nettletown Electric Company clothing and driving an Electric Company van. After passing several "No Trespassing" signs, gates and fences, as well as a sign which said "The Rancho," Officer Snopt reached the suspect area. Remaining in constant radio contact with cover officers, Snopt walked toward the main building. He saw a number of people walking from one building to another or talking in groups of two or three. Officer Snopt took readings from the meter and then attempted to inspect several of the outbuildings. He was abruptly steered from that area, but not before seeing a number of cardboard boxes stacked as if ready for shipment.

Later consultation with an expert from Nettletown Electric revealed that the power consumption, as revealed by the meter readings, was eight times greater than would be expected from the dairy or light industry that occupies that section of Nettletown County. At this point, TFTF determined to obtain a search warrant for "The Rancho."

Superior Court of the State of
Cascadia

_____ COUNTY OF NETTLE _____

TO: Custodian of Records
Bank of Nettle
714 No. 1st
Nettletown, Cascadia   00077

SUBPOENA TO TESTIFY BEFORE GRAND JURY

SUBPOENA FOR
[X] PERSON   [X] DOCUMENT(S) OR OBJECTS

YOU ARE HEREBY COMMANDED to appear and testify before the Grand Jury of the State of Cascadia Superior Court at the place, date, and time specified below

PLACE	COURTROOM
NETTLETOWN COURTHOUSE	#7
	DATE AND TIME
	12/8/Y-1/ 9:00 A.M.

YOU ARE ALSO COMMANDED to bring with you the following document(s) or object(s):*

All records and documents concerning the Bank of Nettlecard
account of **GILBERT J. JARDINE**, 2157 Cherry Ave, Nettletown, from
1/1/Y-1 to 11/24/Y-1

[ ] _Please see additional information on reverse_

This subpoena shall remain in effect until you are granted leave to depart by the court or by an officer acting on behalf of the court.

CLERK	DATE
_Lw_	11/24/Y-1
(BY) DEPUTY CLERK	

This Subpoena is issued on application of the Nettletown County Prosecutor	NAME, ADDRESS AND PHONE NUMBER DEPUTY PROSECUTOR
	Kathryn Q. McManis

* IF NOT APPLICABLE, EN~~~~~~~

APPENDIX S

INVESTIGATION REPORT
AGENCY:
[ ] NPD [X] TFTF

Page 1 of 2

1	Public Disclosure Act	OTHER:

2 Arrest	3 Vehicle	4 Juvenile	8 Report Name/Offense
5 Property	6 Medical	7 Domestic Viol	TAPE FRAUD INVESTIGATION

9 Type of Premise (For vehicles, state where parked.)	10 Entry Point	11 Method

12 Weapon/Tool/Force Used	13 Date Reported 12.9.4-1	14 Time Reported	15 Date Occurrence	16 Time Occurrence	17 Day of Week
				19 Census	20 Dist.

18 Location of: Incident [ ] Address [ ]

PERSONS/BUSINESS INVOLVED

CODE C (Person Reporting Complaint) V (Victim) W (Witness) P (Parent) VB (Victim Business) O (Other)

21 Code	22 NAME: Last	First	Middle (Maiden)	23 Race/Sex	24 Date of Birth	25 Home Phone
26 DPA	27 ADDRESS: Street	City	State Zip	28 Place of Employment/School		29 Business Phone
21 Code	22 NAME: Last	First	Middle (Maiden)	23 Race/Sex	24 Date of Birth	25 Home Phone
26 DPA	27 ADDRESS: Street	City	State Zip	28 Place of Employment/School		29 Business Phone
21 Code	22 NAME: Last	First	Middle (Maiden)	23 Race/Sex	24 Date of Birth	25 Home Phone
26 DPA	27 ADDRESS: Street	City	State Zip	28 Place of Employment/School		29 Business Phone

[ ] Additional persons on Report Continuation Sheet (People) Form No. Z-556

PERSON NUMBER 1

CODE: A (Arrest) S (Suspect) SV (Suspect Verified) R (Runaway) M (Missing Person) I (Institutional Impact)

30 Code	31 NAME: Last	First	Middle (Maiden)	32 Home Phone	33 Business Phone
S	JARDINE	GILBERT	J		
34 ADDRESS: Street	City	State Zip	35 Occupation	36 Place of Employment/School	37 Relation to Victim
2157 CHERRY AVE.	NETTLETOWN	00071			

38 Date of Birth	39 Race	40 Sex	41 Height	42 Weight/Build	43 Hair	44 Eyes	45 Clothing, Scars, marks, Tattoos, Peculiarities, A.K.A.

46 Number	47 Charge Details (Include Ordinance or R.C.W. Number)
[ ] Booked [ ] Cited	

PERSON NUMBER 2

30 Code	31 NAME: Last	First	Middle (Maiden)	32 Home Phone	33 Business Phone

34 ADDRESS: Street	City	State Zip	35 Occupation	36 Place of Employment/School	37 Relation to Victim

38 Date of Birth	39 Race	40 Sex	41 Height	42 Weight/Build	43 Hair	44 Eyes	45 Clothing, Scars, marks, Tattoos, Peculiarities, A.K.A.

46 Number	47 Charge Details (Include Ordinance or R.C.W. Number)
[ ] Booked [ ] Cited	

[ ] Additional persons on Report Continuation Sheet (People) Form No. Z-556   Juvenile Arrests - Block No. 109 MUST Be completed

VEHICLE

48 Stolen	49 Victim	50 Impound	54 License No.	55 Lic/State	56 Lic/Year	57 Lic/Type	58 Vin.
51 Recovery	52 Suspect	53 Hold					
59 Year	60 Make	61 Model	62 Body Style	63 Color	64 Peculiarities	65 Hold Requested by/For	

66 Ori. & Case No.	67 Registered Owner: Name	Address	City	State Zip	68 Home Phone

69 Condition [ ] Drivable [ ] Not Drivable [ ] Stripped [ ] Wrecked	70 Inventory		
70 Inventory (Continued)		71 Tow Co. & Signature	

72 Enter	73 Date	74 Time	75 WACIC	76 LESA	77 Initial	78 Release Info	79 Date	80 Time	81 Release No.	82 Releasing Authority
83 Clear	84	85	86	87	88	89 Owner Notified	90	91	92 Operator's Name	

93 Signature & I.D. No. of Reporting Officer(s)	94 Approval	95 Distribution Excp.
A. Morris (#301)		
REPORT PROCESSING (Records Personnel Only) DISTRIBUTION: DATE ____ BY ____ INDEXED: DATE ____ BY ____	Microfilmed Initials ____	Filed Initials ____

C3:\C\PJ\POLICE.RPT

APPENDIX T

NARRATIVE

On October 9, Y-1, officers of the TFTF took the Bank of NettleCard receipts found in the Camaro to the bank of Nettle, seeking to obtain the NettleCard records of Gilbert Jardine. Bank of Nettle refused to surrender this evidence without a court order, as was their policy.

RO then sought the assistance of the District Attorney of Nettletown who was already in the process of directing a grand jury investigation of cassette tape "bootlegging." At her request, on November 24, Y-1, the grand jury issued a subpoena for the NettleCard records. The bank was served with the subpoena and complied by producing the records on December 9, Y-1. According to the records, the cardholder, Gilbert Jardine, had purchased over $20,000 worth of recording equipment over the past eight months in addition to some 30 older model cars like the suspect Camaro and Cougar.

1

2

3

4

5

6

STATE OF CASCADIA   )
County of Nettle   )   NO. SW 1542
)
_____)

7

8

THE STATE of CASCADIA

TO: The sheriff or any peace officer of said county:

9

10

11

12

13

14

15

WHEREAS, Detective Austin Morris #301 has this day made complaint on oath to the undersigned one of the judges of the above entitled court in and for said county that on or about 9th day of November, Y-1, in Nettle County, Cascadia, a felony, to-wit: CONSPIRACY TO PRODUCE AND DISTRIBUTE UNAUTHORIZED COPYRIGHTED MATERIAL was committed, and that the following evidence, to-wit:

16

17

18

19

20

21

22

23

24

25

26

1.   "Bootleg" tapes, tape masters, blank cassettes, packaging, labels, recording machines and equipment, ledgers, records of bills, correspondence concerning these activities, receipts, personal property or possessions of Gilbert Jardine, Boyd Stern, Miller Frone, William Bean, or James Dailey, Bank of NettleCard slips, large amounts of cash, phone bills, electric bills, and all other papers relating to the illegal duplication and distribution of bootleg tapes.

27

28

SEARCH WARRANT
   (Evidence)
Page 1 of 3
C:\CP\SH-WARNT.DOC

APPENDIX U

2.   Indicia of occupancy, residency, and/or ownership of the premises described in the Search Warrant, including but not limited to, utility and telephone bills, canceled envelopes, and keys.

Is material to the investigation and prosecution of the above described felony and that said Detective Austin Morris #301 verily believes said evidence is concealed in or about a large wooden main building, as well as all out-buildings, on a residence known as "THE RANCHO" which is located one mile east of Pine Road on Big Tree Road.

THEREFORE, in the name of the State of Cascadia, you are commanded that within ten days from this date, with necessary and proper assistance, you enter into and/or search the said house, person, place or thing, to-wit: a large wooden main building, as well as all out-buildings, on a residence known as "THE RANCHO" which is located one mile east of Pine Road on Big Tree Road.

A SEARCH IS TO INCLUDE THE FOLLOWING:

1)   The curtilege of the described Rancho.

2)   The persons of Gil Jardine, Boyd Stern, Miller Frone, William Bean, James Dailey, or any other persons entering, leaving, or on said premises at the time of the search.

And then and there diligently search for said evidence, and any other, and if same, or evidence material to the investigation or prosecution of said felony or any part thereof, be found on such search, bring the same forthwith before me. To be disposed of according to law. A copy of this warrant shall be served upon the person or persons found in or on said house or place and if no person is found in or on said house or place, a copy of this warrant shall be posted upon any conspicuous place in or on said house, place, or thing and a copy of this warrant and inventory shall be returned to the undersigned judge or his agent promptly after execution. **BAIL TO BE SET IN OPEN COURT.**

_____ This warrant is to be served only during the day. [I.e., 6 a.m. to 6 p.m.]

___X___ This warrant may be served day or night.

GIVEN UNDER MY HAND this 15th day of November, Y-1.

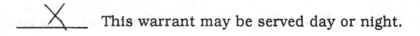

RE Emory
JUDGE

SEARCH WARRANT
(Evidence)
Page 3 of 3
C:\C\P\\SH-WARNT.DOC

IN THE SUPERIOR COURT OF THE STATE OF CASCADIA
FOR NETTLE COUNTY
COMPLAINT FOR SEARCH WARRANT
(Evidence)

STATE OF CASCADIA　　　　)
County of Nettle　　　　　　)　　　　　　　NO. SW 1542
_____)

I, AUSTIN MORRIS, am the affiant for this Complaint for Search Warrant. I

have been a police officer in the City of Nettletown for 19 years. For the last three years I

have been assigned as a detective to the Tape Fraud Task Force [TFTF], a statewide task

force of peace officers charged with stemming the illegal flow of fraudulently copied video

and audio cassette tapes. After receiving three weeks of intensive training by the FBI in

investigating "bootleg tape" cases, I have participated in over 150 arrests and over 200

separate investigations involving the illegal manufacturing and sale of copyrighted cassette

tape material.

Probable cause to search a large wooden main building, as well as all outbuildings,

on a residence known as "The Rancho" which is located one mile east of Pine Road on

Big Tree Road, is based on the following:

On 10/06/Y-1, your affiant received information from Officer Dubow (Badge

#642) that a reliable confidential informant had told him that a large bootleg tape

operation was being conducted from a location known as "The Rancho" in the Big Tree

Area, and that the operation was run by a man named "Gil." This informant has previously

provided information leading to the arrest and conviction of two drug suspects.

On 09/15/Y-1, a search of a Y-10 Mercury Cougar rented by one Gilbert Jardine

had disclosed two cartons of cassette tapes which TFTF acoustics expert, Sally Sands,

determined to be unauthorized recordings of live rock concerts throughout the state. A

postcard found in the booking search of the driver of a Y-10 Camaro, also rented by

APPENDIX V

Jardine, indicated that "The stuff is ready at The Rancho for you to pick up ... it's real hiiigh fidelity!!!" and was signed "Gil."

On 10/30/Y-1, helicopter surveillance over the Big Tree area located a series of camouflaged buildings hidden in the trees. The location of these buildings corresponded to a hand-drawn map found, wrapped around a bootleg cassette, during the 09/09/Y-1 search of a passenger in the same Y-10 Camaro rented by Gilbert Jardine.

Subsequent satellite surveillance revealed a main building, four outbuildings, several people around the main building, and a number of trucks. Cartons similar to ones found in the Cougar appeared about to be loaded into the trucks.

On 11/09/Y-1, Officer Snopt of the TFTF entered the surveilled property on foot, posing as a meterman for the local electric company. He saw a sign at the entrance that said "Rancho." As he walked past the main building, he saw a number of cartons similar to the ones found in the Camaro stacked up as if they were about to be transported. He was quickly stopped from going further into this area of the property by several unidentified person. Snopt then took a meter reading which, according to experts at the utility who we subsequently consulted, was eight (8) times the use one would normally expect from such property with normal use.

Based upon the foregoing and my experience and training as a police officer dealing with the fraudulent manufacture and distribution of copyrighted material, I have probable cause to believe that the illegal manufacture of cassette tapes is being done in the five buildings located one mile east of Pine Road on Big Tree Road and that a search of that residence will reveal bootleg tapes and the supplies and equipment for producing such tapes, as well as evidence revealing the identity of members of the illegal operation.

I declare the foregoing to be true and correct under penalty of perjury.

Dated October 15, 19Y-0   Signed _Austin Morris_____
                                        Austin Morris (Badge #301)
                                        Affiant Detective

COMPLAINT FOR SEARCH WARRANT
(Evidence)
Page 2 of 2

RETURN OF OFFICER

STATE OF CASCADIA   )   **No. SW 1542**

)   **ss**

County of Nettle   )

      THIS IS TO CERTIFY that I received the within Search Warrant on the 15th day of November, Y-1, and that pursuant to the command contained therein, I made due and diligent search of the property described therein and found the following:

- 2 AKAI highspeed duplicating machines
- 700 gross blank tapes
- 5,000 copies duplicated tapes
- 2 Farnsworth Labeling Machines
- .22 rifle
- Shotgun
- Blank label
- Packing Cartons
- Correspondence to Gil Jardine
- Purchase receipts
- Letters, bills etc. of Ralph Freely
- 8 x 10 photograph

Names of persons found in possession of property: _____

     Gil Jardine, Ralph Freely, Rachel Klein, Kevin Lumus,

     Edward Broil

RETURN OF OFFICE
Page 1 of 2
C2\CP\\ROF.DOC

APPENDIX W

Names of persons served with true and complete copy of Search Warrant:

_____

_____ NONE _____

_____

Description of door or conspicuous place where copy of Search Warrant posted:

_____ Kitchen table of main building _____

_____

Place where property is now kept:

_____ Nettletown police department property room _____

_____

Dated this 15th day of December, Y-1.

Witness: M. Austin #301

APPENDIX X

ARREST REPORT

AGENCY: [ ] NPD   [ ] TFTF

Page 1 of 4

Page 1 of 4

1	Public Disclosure Act	OTHER: _____	

2 Arrest	X 3 Vehicle	4 Juvenile	8 Report Name/Offense
5 Property	6 Medical	7 Domestic Viol	TAPE FRAUD / POSSESS - CONSPIRACY

9 Type of Premise (For vehicles, state where parked.) FARM	10 Entry Point	11 Method

12 Weapon/Tool/Force Used	13 Date Reported 11·27·Y-1	14 Time Reported 0700	15 Date Occurrence	16 Time Occurrence	17 Day of Week

18 Location of Incident [ ] Address [ ]	"THE RANCHO" 1 mile east of Pine on Big Tree Road / Incident to executing search warrant	19 Census	20 Dist.

PERSONS/BUSINESS INVOLVED

CODE   C (Person Reporting Complaint)   V (Victim)   W (Witness)   P (Parent)   VB (Victim Business)   O (Other)

21 Code	22 NAME: Last	First	Middle (Maiden)	23 Race/Sex	24 Date of Birth	25 Home Phone
26 DPA	27 ADDRESS: Street	City	State	Zip	28 Place of Employment/School	29 Business Phone

21 Code	22 NAME: Last	First	Middle (Maiden)	23 Race/Sex	24 Date of Birth	25 Home Phone
26 DPA	27 ADDRESS: Street	City	State	Zip	28 Place of Employment/School	29 Business Phone

21 Code	22 NAME: Last	First	Middle (Maiden)	23 Race/Sex	24 Date of Birth	25 Home Phone
26 DPA	27 ADDRESS: Street	City	State	Zip	28 Place of Employment/School	29 Business Phone

[ ] Additional persons on Report Continuation Sheet (People) Form No. Z-556

CODE: A (Arrest)   S (Suspect)   SV (Suspect Verified)   R (Runaway)   M (Missing Person)   I (Institutional Impact)

PERSON NUMBER 1

30 Code A.	31 NAME: Last JARDINE	First GILBERT	Middle (Maiden) J.	32 Home Phone	33 Business Phone

34 ADDRESS: Street 2157 CHERRY AVE	City NETTLETOWN	State	Zip 00071	35 Occupation CONTRACTOR	36 Place of Employment/School SELF-EMPLOYED	37 Relation to Victim

38 Date of Birth 10.15.Y-46	39 Race C	40 Sex M	41 Height 6'	42 Weight/Build 210 lbs	43 Hair blonde	44 Eyes blue	45 Clothing, Scars, marks, Tattoos, Peculiarities, A.K.A. tatoo of "Mother" on back of hand

46 ☒ Booked [ ] Cited Number	47 Charge Details (Include Ordinance or R.C.W. Number) 9.777 (conspiracy) 15.006(d) (possess. of bootleg tapes)

PERSON NUMBER 2

30 Code A.	31 NAME: Last FREELY	First RALPH	Middle (Maiden) NMI	32 Home Phone	33 Business Phone

34 ADDRESS: Street "THE RANCHO"	City	State	Zip	35 Occupation CARETAKER	36 Place of Employment/School THE RANCHO	37 Relation to Victim

38 Date of Birth 2.7.Y-22	39 Race HISP	40 Sex M	41 Height 5'10"	42 Weight/Build 165 lbs	43 Hair short brn	44 Eyes brn.	45 Clothing, Scars, marks, Tattoos, Peculiarities, A.K.A.

46 ☒ Booked [ ] Cited Number	47 Charge Details (Include Ordinance or R.C.W. Number) 9.777 (conspiracy) 15.006(d) (possess. of bootleg tapes)

[ ] Additional persons on Report Continuation Sheet (People) Form No. Z-556   Juvenile Arrests - Block No. 109 MUST Be completed

VEHICLE

48 Stolen	49 Victim	50 Impound	54 License No.	55 Lic/State	56 Lic/Year	57 Lic/Type	58 Vin.
51 Recovery	52 Suspect	53 Hold					

59 Year	60 Make	61 Model	62 Body Style	63 Color	64 Peculiarities	65 Hold Requested by/For

66 Ori. & Case No.	67 Registered Owner: Name	Address	City	State	Zip	68 Home Phone

69 Condition [ ] Drivable [ ] Not Drivable [ ] Stripped [ ] Wrecked	70 Inventory

70 Inventory (Continued)	71 Tow Co. & Signature

72 Enter	73 Date	74 Time	75 WACIC	76 LESA	77 Initial	78 Release Info	79 Date	80 Time	81 Release No.	82 Releasing Authority
83 Clear	84	85	86	87	88	89 Owner Notified	90	91	92 Operator's Name	

93 Signature & I.D. No. of Reporting Officer(s) A. Morris (# 301)	94 Approval	95 Distribution Excp.

REPORT PROCESSING (Records Personnel Only)	DISTRIBUTION: DATE _____ BY _____ INDEXED: DATE _____ BY _____	Microfilmed Initials_____	Filed Initials_____

C3:\C\PJ\POLICE.RPT

APPENDIX Y

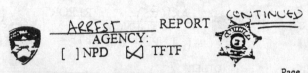

ARREST REPORT (CONTINUED)

AGENCY:
[ ] NPD [X] TFTF

Page 2 of 4

1 Public Disclosure Act	OTHER: _____	

2 Arrest	[✓] 3 Vehicle	4 Juvenile	8 Report Name/Offense	
5 Property	6 Medical	7 Domestic Viol		

9 Type of Premise (For vehicles, state where parked.)	10 Entry Point	11 Method

12 Weapon /Tool/Force Used	13 Date Reported	14 Time Reported	15 Date Occurrence	16 Time Occurrence	17 Day of Week

18 Location of: Incident [ ] Address [ ]	SEARCH WARRANT FOR "THE RANCHO"	19 Census	20 Dist.

PERSONS/BUSINESS INVOLVED

CODE C (Person Reporting Complaint) V (Victim) W (Witness) P (Parent) VB (Victim Business) O (Other)

21 Code	22 NAME: Last	First	Middle (Maiden)	23 Race/Sex	24 Date of Birth	25 Home Phone
26 DPA	27 ADDRESS: Street	City	State	Zip	28 Place of Employment/School	29 Business Phone
21 Code	22 NAME: Last	First	Middle (Maiden)	23 Race/Sex	24 Date of Birth	25 Home Phone
26 DPA	27 ADDRESS: Street	City	State	Zip	28 Place of Employment/School	29 Business Phone
21 Code	22 NAME: Last	First	Middle (Maiden)	23 Race/Sex	24 Date of Birth	25 Home Phone
26 DPA	27 ADDRESS: Street	City	State	Zip	28 Place of Employment/School	29 Business Phone

[ ] Additional persons on Report Continuation Sheet (People) Form No. Z-556

CODE: A (Arrest) S (Suspect) SV (Suspect Verified) R (Runaway) M (Missing Person) I (Institutional Impact)

PERSON NUMBER 3

30 Code	31 NAME: Last	First	Middle (Maiden)		32 Home Phone	33 Business Phone
A	KLEIN	RACHEL	R			
34 ADDRESS: Street	City	State	Zip	35 Occupation	36 Place of Employment/School	37 Relation to Victim
HARBOR ARTS (#206) 15 RIDGEVIEW DR.	NETTLETOWN		00072	PAINTER	SELF-EMPLOYED	
38 Date of Birth	39 Race	40 Sex	41 Height	42 Weight/Build	43 Hair blk (skkushd)	44 Eyes blk	45 Clothing, Scars, marks, Tattoos, Peculiarities, A.K.A.
5·29·Y-22	C	F	5'7"	122 lbs			
46 [✓]Booked [ ]Cited Number	47 Charge Details (Include Ordinance or R.C.W. Number) 9.777 (conspiracy) 15.006(d) (possen. of bootleg tapes)					

PERSON NUMBER 4

30 Code	31 NAME: Last	First	Middle (Maiden)		32 Home Phone	33 Business Phone
A	LUMUS	KEVIN	M			
34 ADDRESS: Street	City	State	Zip	35 Occupation	36 Place of Employment/School	37 Relation to Victim
200 HAMPTON ST.	SO. CITY		00059	HORSE TRAINER	SELF-EMPLOYED	
38 Date of Birth	39 Race	40 Sex	41 Height	42 Weight/Build	43 Hair brn	44 Eyes brn	45 Clothing, Scars, marks, Tattoos, Peculiarities, A.K.A.
11·11·Y-29	C	M	5'11"	137 lbs			
46 [✓]Booked [ ]Cited Number	47 Charge Details (Include Ordinance or R.C.W. Number) 9.777 (conspiracy) 15.006(d) (possess. of bootleg tapes)					

[ ] Additional persons on Report Continuation Sheet (People) Form No. Z-556   Juvenile Arrests - Block No. 109 MUST Be completed

VEHICLE

48 Stolen	49 Victim	50 Impound	54 License No.	55 Lic/State	56 Lic/Year	57 Lic/Type	58 Vin.
51 Recovery	52 Suspect	53 Hold					
59 Year	60 Make	61 Model	62 Body Style	63 Color	64 Peculiarities	65 Hold Requested by/For	

66 Ori. & Case No.	67 Registered Owner: Name	Address	City	State	Zip	68 Home Phone

69 Condition [ ] Drivable [ ] Not Drivable [ ] Stripped [ ] Wrecked	70 Inventory

70 Inventory (Continued)	71 Tow Co. & Signature

72 Enter	73 Date	74 Time	75 WACIC	76 LESA	77 Initial	78 Release Info	79 Date	80 Time	81 Release No.	82 Releasing Authority
83 Clear	84	85	86	87	88	89 Owner Notified	90	91	92 Operator's Name	

93 Signature & I.D. No. of Reporting Officer(s)	94 Approval	95 Distribution Excp.

REPORT PROCESSING (Records Personnel Only)	DISTRIBUTION: DATE _____ BY _____ INDEXED: DATE _____ BY _____	Microfilmed Initials_____	Filed Initials_____

C3:\C\P\\POLICE.RPT

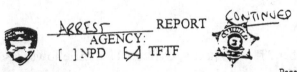

1 Public Disclosure Act					
2 Arrest	✗ 3 Vehicle	4 Juvenile		8 Report Name/Offense	
5 Property	6 Medical	7 Domestic Viol			
9 Type of Premise (For vehicles, state where parked.)			10 Entry Point		11 Method
12 Weapon /Tool/Force Used			13 Date Reported	14 Time Reported	15 Date Occurrence	16 Time Occurrence	17 Day of Week

18 Location of: Incident [ ] Address [ ] RANCHO SEARCH | 19 Census | 20 Dist. |

PERSONS/BUSINESS INVOLVED

CODE	C (Person Reporting Complaint)	V (Victim)	W (Witness)	P (Parent)	VB (Victim Business)	O (Other)
21 Code	22 NAME: Last First		Middle (Maiden)	23 Race/Sex	24 Date of Birth	25 Home Phone
26 DPA	27 ADDRESS: Street City		State Zip	28 Place of Employment/School		29 Business Phone
21 Code	22 NAME: Last First		Middle (Maiden)	23 Race/Sex	24 Date of Birth	25 Home Phone
26 DPA	27 ADDRESS: Street City		State Zip	28 Place of Employment/School		29 Business Phone
21 Code	22 NAME: Last First		Middle (Maiden)	23 Race/Sex	24 Date of Birth	25 Home Phone
26 DPA	27 ADDRESS: Street City		State Zip	28 Place of Employment/School		29 Business Phone

[ ] Additional persons on Report Continuation Sheet (People) Form No. Z-556

PERSON NUMBER 1

CODE: A (Arrest)   S (Suspect)   SV (Suspect Verified)   R (Runaway)   M (Missing Person)   I (Institutional Impact)

30 Code	31 NAME: Last First Middle (Maiden)			32 Home Phone	33 Business Phone
A	BROIL EDWARD G.				
34 ADDRESS: Street City State Zip	35 Occupation	36 Place of Employment/School	37 Relation to Victim
90210 Melrose Pl. Northtown 00071	SHEET ROCKER	SELF-EMPLOYED	
38 Date of Birth	39 Race	40 Sex	41 Height	42 Weight/Build	43 Hair	44 Eyes	45 Clothing, Scars, marks, Tattoos, Peculiarities, A.K.A.
4.13.4-45	C	M	6'1"	155 lbs	Red curley	blue	beard
46 ☒ Booked [ ] Cited Number	47 Charge Details (Include Ordinance or R.C.W. Number)				
	9.777 (conspiracy) 15.0061d) (possession of booby traps)				

PERSON NUMBER 2

30 Code	31 NAME: Last First Middle (Maiden)			32 Home Phone	33 Business Phone
34 ADDRESS: Street City State Zip	35 Occupation	36 Place of Employment/School	37 Relation to Victim
38 Date of Birth	39 Race	40 Sex	41 Height	42 Weight/Build	43 Hair	44 Eyes	45 Clothing, Scars, marks, Tattoos, Peculiarities, A.K.A.
46 [ ] Booked [ ] Cited Number	47 Charge Details (Include Ordinance or R.C.W. Number)				

[ ] Additional persons on Report Continuation Sheet (People) Form No. Z-556   Juvenile Arrests - Block No. 109 MUST Be completed

VEHICLE

48 Stolen	49 Victim	50 Impound	54 License No.	55 Lic/State	56 Lic/Year	57 Lic/Type	58 Vin.
51 Recovery	52 Suspect	53 Hold					
59 Year	60 Make	61 Model	62 Body Style	63 Color	64 Peculiarities	65 Hold Requested by/For	
66 Ori. & Case No.	67 Registered Owner: Name		Address	City	State	Zip	68 Home Phone

69 Condition [ ] Drivable [ ] Stripped [ ] Not Drivable [ ] Wrecked	70 Inventory
70 Inventory (Continued)	71 Tow Co. & Signature

72 Enter	73 Date	74 Time	75 WACIC	76 LESA	77 Initial	78 Release Info	79 Date	80 Time	81 Release No.	82 Releasing Authority
83 Clear	84	85	86	87	88	89 Owner Notified	90	91	92 Operator's Name	

93 Signature & I.D. No. of Reporting Officer(s)	94 Approval	95 Distribution Excp.

REPORT PROCESSING (Records Personnel Only)	DISTRIBUTION: DATE _____ BY _____ INDEXED: DATE _____ BY _____	Microfilmed Initials_____	Filed Initials_____

C3:\C\P\\POLICE.RPT

NARRATIVE

On November 27, 0700 hours, Officers Henry Fellows, Jay Johnson, Dale Snopt and RO of the Tape Fraud Task Force, together with seventeen officers of the Nettletown Police Department, served Search Warrant #1542 on the suspect "The Rancho."

Officer Fellows and RO entered the main building at 0700 hours. In the building were GIL JARDINE, RACHEL KLEIN, EDWARD BROIL, and KEVIN LUMUS. These persons were detained without incident. We immediately found two AKAI high-speed cassette duplicating machines together with 200 gross of blank cassette tapes and about 5,000 copies of an illegally recorded "Macho Wimps" concert. In addition, we found one .22 rifle and a shotgun. Searches of the various other buildings produced two labeling machines, 500 gross of blank labels, one gross of "Macho Wimps" labels, sales and purchase receipts for blank tapes in the name of Top Music, Inc., and various other items and paraphernalia associated with the manufacture and sale of bootleg tapes.

About 300 yards from the main building, hidden in the trees, Officer Snopt discovered a small, single-room cabin with an Indian bedspread over the doorway. Immediately prior to entry, Officer Snopt heard "muffled sounds" and something like the word "cop." Upon entering the cabin, Officer Snopt found suspect RALPH FREELY seated next to a table on which was placed a framed 8" x 10" glossy photograph of three men in bowling shirts with a trophy. The names embroidered on the shirts were "Ralph," "Cal," and "T.C.," respectively, left to right. Suspect Freely was the person pictured on the left. Other letters and phone bills found in the cabin confirmed that Freely was the regular occupant.

Jardine, Klein, Broil, Lumus, and Freely were placed under arrest and transported for booking.

ARREST REPORT

AGENCY:
[ ] NPD   [ ] TFTF

OTHER: _____

Page 1 of 3

1 Public Disclosure Act				
2 Arrest	☒ 3 Vehicle	4 Juvenile	8 Report Name/Offense	
5 Property	6 Medical	7 Domestic Viol	THE FRAU(1)	
9 Type of Premise (For vehicles, state where parked.)		10 Entry Point		11 Method
12 Weapon/Tool/Force Used		13 Date Reported 11·27·Y·1	14 Time Reported 0745	15 Date Occurrence 11·27·Y·1 16 Time Occurrence 0745 17 Day of Week

18 Location of: Incident Address	☒ BIGTREE ROAD ["ROADBLOCK"]	19 Census	20 Dist.

PERSONS/BUSINESS INVOLVED

CODE C (Person Reporting Complaint) V (Victim) W (Witness) P (Parent) VB (Victim Business) O (Other)

21 Code	22 NAME: Last First Middle (Maiden)	23 Race/Sex	24 Date of Birth	25 Home Phone
26 DPA	27 ADDRESS: Street City State Zip	28 Place of Employment/School		29 Business Phone
21 Code	22 NAME: Last First Middle (Maiden)	23 Race/Sex	24 Date of Birth	25 Home Phone
26 DPA	27 ADDRESS: Street City State Zip	28 Place of Employment/School		29 Business Phone
21 Code	22 NAME: Last First Middle (Maiden)	23 Race/Sex	24 Date of Birth	25 Home Phone
26 DPA	27 ADDRESS: Street City State Zip	28 Place of Employment/School		29 Business Phone

[ ] Additional persons on Report Continuation Sheet (People) Form No. Z-556

CODE: A (Arrest) S (Suspect) SV (Suspect Verified) R (Runaway) M (Missing Person) I (Institutional Impact)

PERSON NUMBER 1

30 Code A	31 NAME: Last BEAN First WILLIAM Middle (Maiden) J.		32 Home Phone	33 Business Phone
34 ADDRESS: Street CRESTVIEW APTS #601 531 CRESTVIEW AVE	City NETTLETOWN	State	Zip 00072	35 Occupation PLUMBER	36 Place of Employment/School SELF-EMPLOYED	37 Relation to Victim
38 Date of Birth 9-1-Y-26	39 Race C	40 Sex M	41 Height 6'2"	42 Weight/Build 195 lbs	43 Hair BRN	44 Eyes BRN	45 Clothing, Scars, marks, Tattoos, Peculiarities, A.K.A. PONYTAIL
46 ☒ Booked [ ] Cited Number	47 Charge Details (Include Ordinance or R.C.W. Number) 15.006(d) (POSSESS. OF BOOTLEG TAPES)			

PERSON NUMBER 2

30 Code	31 NAME: Last First Middle (Maiden)		32 Home Phone	33 Business Phone
34 ADDRESS: Street	City State Zip	35 Occupation	36 Place of Employment/School	37 Relation to Victim
38 Date of Birth	39 Race	40 Sex	41 Height	42 Weight/Build	43 Hair	44 Eyes	45 Clothing, Scars, marks, Tattoos, Peculiarities, A.K.A.
46 [ ] Booked [ ] Cited Number	47 Charge Details (Include Ordinance or R.C.W. Number)			

[ ] Additional persons on Report Continuation Sheet (People) Form No. Z-556   Juvenile Arrests - Block No. 109 MUST Be completed

VEHICLE

48 Stolen	49 Victim	50 Impound ☒	54 License No. BUH-707	55 Lic/State	56 Lic/Year Y-1	57 Lic/Type	58 Vin.
51 Recovery	52 Suspect ☒	53 Hold					
59 Year Y-5	60 Make PONTIAC	61 Model FIREBIRD	62 Body Style	63 Color RED	64 Peculiarities	65 Hold Requested by/For	
66 Ori. & Case No.	67 Registered Owner: Name WILLIAM BEAN (SEE ABOVE) Address City State Zip						68 Home Phone
69 Condition [ ] Drivable [ ] Stripped [ ] Not Drivable [ ] Wrecked		70 Inventory (SEE ATTACHED SHEET)					
70 Inventory (Continued)				71 Tow Co. & Signature			

72 Enter	73 Date	74 Time	75 WACIC	76 LESA	77 Initial	78 Release Info	79 Date	80 Time	81 Release No.	82 Releasing Authority
83 Clear	84	85	86	87	88	89 Owner Notified	90	91	92 Operator's Name	

93 Signature & I.D. No. of Reporting Officer(s) #117	94 Approval	95 Distribution Excp.

REPORT PROCESSING (Records Personnel Only)	DISTRIBUTION: DATE _____ BY _____ INDEXED: DATE _____ BY _____	Microfilmed Initials _____	Filed Initials _____

C3:\C\P\\POLICE.RPT

APPENDIX Z

NARRATIVE

At 0735 hours, RO was off duty driving near the "Big Tree" area in his patrol vehicle when he picked up an all points bulletin to "stop all vehicles out of the Big Tree area." At 0745 hours, I saw the same Y-5 Pontiac Firebird, license BUH 707, that I had been following 3 days earlier from the post office being driven by a different driver.

I pulled my car in front of the path of the suspect Pontiac on Pine Road, and displaying my service revolver, ordered the occupant out. With hands in the air, the suspect driver, who identified himself as WILLIAM BEAN, was pat searched for weapons. Though the pat search revealed nothing, under the circumstances of the all points bulletin, I still kept my weapon drawn. I then requested, and suspect Bean consented to, a search of the trunk of the suspect Pontiac. Bean opened the trunk with his keys, revealing two cardboard boxes. I then opened the two cardboard boxes in the trunk. Both boxes were filled with what appeared to be bootleg tapes of the August Nettletown Square Garden concert of the "Aural High Jeanists." Suspect Bean was placed under arrest and the tapes taken into evidence.

PROPERTY REPORT

AGENCY NPD O TFTF Ø OTHER _____ **DATE** 11-27-Y-1.

| PROP ROOM USE ONLY | PAGE 3 of 3 |

TYPE OF CRIME TAPE FRAUD

LABORATORY WORK REQUIRED: YES _____

RELATED CASE NO.

Ø EVIDENCE   O FOUND

O SAFEKEEPING   O OWNER UNKNOWN

| CENSUS | DIST. |

PROPERTY OBTAINED FROM: # PONTIAC FIREBIRD BUH707   ADDRESS   PHONE

VICTIM
| LAST NAME | FIRST | MIDDLE |
| STREET ADDRESS | CITY | PHONE |

SUBJECT
LAST NAME	FIRST	MIDDLE
BEAN	WILLIAM	J.
STREET ADDRESS 3,34 CRESTVIEW APTS. APT. #601 521 CRESTVIEW AVE.	CITY NETTLETOWN	PHONE

PROPERTY INVENTORY

ITEM NO.	PROPERTY DESCRIPTION	QTY	SERIAL NO.	WA NOC	LOCATION	RECEIPT NO.
1	2 BOXES CASSETTE TAPES (CARDBOARD CARTON) - APPROX 2,000 TAPES					

PROPERTY SUBMITTED BY: _H. Williams_ #117   UNIT NO: _____   DATE: 11-27-Y-1

ADDITIONAL DESCRIPTIONS OR COMMENTS:

| IOP ROOM USE ONLY | PROPERTY RECEIVED: METHOD _____ BY: _____ DATE: _____ |
| | PROPERTY INVENTORIED BY: _____ UNIT: _____ DATE: _____ |

C2\CU\PRP-RPT.FRM

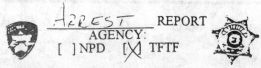

ARREST REPORT

AGENCY:
[ ] NPD [X] TFTF

| 1 Public Disclosure Act | OTHER: _____ | Page _1_ of _3_ |

2 Arrest	X	3 Vehicle		4 Juvenile		8 Report Name/Offense
5 Property		6 Medical		7 Domestic Viol		TAPE FRAUD

9 Type of Premise (For vehicles, state where parked.)	10 Entry Point	11 Method

12 Weapon /Tool/Force Used	13 Date Reported 12-10-Y-1	14 Time Reported 1530	15 Date Occurrence —	16 Time Occurrence	17 Day of Week

18 Location of: Incident [ ] Address [ ]	UNCLE'S HOME WHERE S. STAYING	19 Census	20 Dist.

PERSONS/BUSINESS INVOLVED

CODE   C (Person Reporting Complaint)   V (Victim)   W (Witness)   P (Parent)   VB (Victim Business)   O (Other)

21 Code P(hone)	22 NAME: Last KOGERS	First BEN	Middle (Maiden) F.	23 Race/Sex C	24 Date of Birth 2-3-Y-35	25 Home Phone 641-4140
26 DPA	27 ADDRESS: Street 1544 LOWER CAMP DR.	City NETTLETOWN	State	Zip 00069	28 Place of Employment/School EAGLE GROCERY	29 Business Phone 839-1947
21 Code	22 NAME: Last	First	Middle (Maiden)	23 Race/Sex	24 Date of Birth	25 Home Phone
26 DPA	27 ADDRESS: Street	City	State	Zip	28 Place of Employment/School	29 Business Phone
21 Code	22 NAME: Last	First	Middle (Maiden)	23 Race/Sex	24 Date of Birth	25 Home Phone
26 DPA	27 ADDRESS: Street	City	State	Zip	28 Place of Employment/School	29 Business Phone

[ ] Additional persons on Report Continuation Sheet (People) Form No. Z-556

PERSON NUMBER 1

CODE: A (Arrest)   S (Suspect)   SV (Suspect Verified)   R (Runaway)   M (Missing Person)   I (Institutional Impact)

30 Code A	31 NAME: Last BAILEY	First JAMES	Middle (Maiden) E.	32 Home Phone	33 Business Phone
34 ADDRESS: Street 1544 LOWER CAMP DR.	City NETTLETOWN	State	Zip 00069	35 Occupation STUDENT	36 Place of Employment/School NETTLETOWN H.S.	37 Relation to Victim

38 Date of Birth 88-Y-16	39 Race C	40 Sex M	41 Height 5'9"	42 Weight/Build 160 lbs	43 Hair BLONDE CREWCUT	44 Eyes BLUE	45 Clothing, Scars, marks, Tattoos, Peculiarities, A.K.A.

46 [X] Booked [ ] Cited	Number JUVENILE	47 Charge Details (Include Ordinance or R.C.W. Number)

PERSON NUMBER 2

30 Code	31 NAME: Last	First	Middle (Maiden)	32 Home Phone	33 Business Phone
34 ADDRESS: Street	City	State	Zip	35 Occupation	36 Place of Employment/School	37 Relation to Victim

38 Date of Birth	39 Race	40 Sex	41 Height	42 Weight/Build	43 Hair	44 Eyes	45 Clothing, Scars, marks, Tattoos, Peculiarities, A.K.A.

46 [ ] Booked [ ] Cited	Number	47 Charge Details (Include Ordinance or R.C.W. Number)

[ ] Additional persons on Report Continuation Sheet (People) Form No. Z-556   Juvenile Arrests - Block No. 109 MUST Be completed

VEHICLE

48 Stolen	49 Victim	50 Impound	54 License No.	55 Lic/State	56 Lic/Year	57 Lic/Type	58 Vin.
51 Recovery	52 Suspect	53 Hold					

59 Year	60 Make	61 Model	62 Body Style	63 Color	64 Peculiarities	65 Hold Requested by/For

66 Ori. & Case No.	67 Registered Owner: Name	Address	City	State	Zip	68 Home Phone

69 Condition [ ] Drivable [ ] Not Drivable [ ] Stripped [ ] Wrecked	70 Inventory

70 Inventory (Continued)	71 Tow Co. & Signature

72 Enter	73 Date	74 Time	75 WACIC	76 LESA	77 Initial	78 Release Info	79 Date	80 Time	81 Release No.	82 Releasing Authority
83 Clear	84	85	86	87	88	89 Owner Notified	90	91	92 Operator's Name	

93 Signature & I.D. No. of Reporting Officer(s) #117	94 Approval	95 Distribution Excp.

REPORT PROCESSING (Records Personnel Only)	DISTRIBUTION: DATE _____ BY _____ INDEXED: DATE _____ BY _____	Microfilmed Initials _____	Filed Initials _____

C3:\C\P\\POLICE.RPT

APPENDIX AA

NARRATIVE

At 1530 hours, on or about December 10, based on information from an undercover officer working drug enforcement at Nettletown High School, Officer Sheila Doyle of the TFTF and I went to the home of a juvenile, James Dailey, who the undercover officer said was selling bootleg tapes at the school. The residence turned out to be the home of the juvenile's uncle, Ben Rogers, where the juvenile Dailey had been staying temporarily as a result of the death of his father a month before. When we explained the reason for our presence, Mr. Rogers invited us into his house and took us to the room he said James was occupying. What were apparently James's clothes were in the closet, photos of his family on the desk, and various sports posters taped on the wall.

In the corner of the room was a locked trunk. As we were standing there discussing what Mr. Rogers knew of his nephew and wondering what was in the trunk, the juvenile entered the room protesting our presence. He asked us to leave, but his uncle told him, "Boy, you be quiet now. You give me the key to this here trunk this instant!" The juvenile continued protesting, saying that that was his private trunk and had been a gift from his father, but eventually reached in his pocket and took out a key. When the juvenile withdrew the key from his pants pocket, Mr. Rogers took it and opened the trunk. The trunk contained over 1,000 bootleg tapes of various rock groups.

PROPERTY REPORT

AGENCY   NPD ○   PPF ⊗   OTHER _____   DATE 12.10.4-1

TYPE OF CRIME
Tape Fraud

⊗ EVIDENCE   ○ FOUND

○ SAFEKEEPING   ○ OWNER UNKNOWN

LABORATORY WORK REQUIRED   YES _____

RELATED CASE NO

CENSUS | DIST | PHONE

PROPERTY OBTAINED FROM: *Trunk Locker*   ADDRESS   PHONE

	VICTIM				SUBJECT		
LAST NAME	FIRST	MIDDLE		LAST NAME	FIRST	MIDDLE	
				Dailey,	*James*	*K.*	
STREET ADDRESS	CITY	PHONE		STREET ADDRESS	CITY	PHONE	
				1544 Lower Camp Dr.	*Nettleton*	*527-1617*	

PROPERTY INVENTORY

ITEM NO.	PROPERTY DESCRIPTION	QTY	SERIAL NO.	WA NOC	LOCATION	RECEIPT NO.
1	*Cassette tapes of concerts*	1,000				

PROPERTY ROOM USE ONLY

PROPERTY SUBMITTERD BY: *S. Doyle (#714)*   UNIT NO: _____   DATE: *12.10.4-1*

ADDITIONAL DESCRIPTIONS OR COMMENTS:

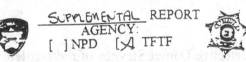

SUPPLEMENTAL REPORT

AGENCY:

[ ] NPD [X] TFTF

1	Public Disclosure Act	OTHER: _____	Page 1 of 2

2 Arrest	3 Vehicle	4 Juvenile	8 Report Name/Offense	
5 Property	6 Medical	7 Domestic Viol		

9 Type of Premise (For vehicles, state where parked.)	10 Entry Point	11 Method

12 Weapon /Tool/Force Used	13 Date Reported 12.14.Y-1	14 Time Reported	15 Date Occurrence	16 Time Occurrence	17 Day of Week

18 Location of: Incident [ ] Address [ ]		19 Census	20 Dist.

PERSONS/BUSINESS INVOLVED

CODE   C (Person Reporting Complaint)   V (Victim)   W (Witness)   P (Parent)   VB (Victim Business)   O (Other)

21 Code	22 NAME: Last	First	Middle (Maiden)	23 Race/Sex	24 Date of Birth	25 Home Phone
26 DPA	27 ADDRESS: Street	City	State Zip	28 Place of Employment/School		29 Business Phone
21 Code	22 NAME: Last	First	Middle (Maiden)	23 Race/Sex	24 Date of Birth	25 Home Phone
26 DPA	27 ADDRESS: Street	City	State Zip	28 Place of Employment/School		29 Business Phone
21 Code	22 NAME: Last	First	Middle (Maiden)	23 Race/Sex	24 Date of Birth	25 Home Phone
26 DPA	27 ADDRESS: Street	City	State Zip	28 Place of Employment/School		29 Business Phone

[ ] Additional persons on Report Continuation Sheet (People) Form No. Z-556

CODE: A (Arrest)   S (Suspect)   SV (Suspect Verified)   R (Runaway)   M (Missing Person)   I (Institutional Impact)

PERSON NUMBER 1

30 Code	31 NAME: Last DAILEY First JAMES Middle (Maiden) E.	32 Home Phone	33 Business Phone
34 ADDRESS: Street 1544 LOWER CAMP Dr. City Nettletown State Zip 00069	35 Occupation	36 Place of Employment/School	37 Relation to Victim
38 Date of Birth	39 Race	40 Sex	41 Height	42 Weight/Build	43 Hair	44 Eyes	45 Clothing, Scars, marks, Tattoos, Peculiarities, A.K.A.
46 [ ] Booked [ ] Cited Number	47 Charge Details (Include Ordinance or R.C.W. Number)

PERSON NUMBER 2

30 Code	31 NAME: Last First Middle (Maiden)	32 Home Phone	33 Business Phone
34 ADDRESS: Street City State Zip	35 Occupation	36 Place of Employment/School	37 Relation to Victim
38 Date of Birth	39 Race	40 Sex	41 Height	42 Weight/Build	43 Hair	44 Eyes	45 Clothing, Scars, marks, Tattoos, Peculiarities, A.K.A.
46 [ ] Booked [ ] Cited Number	47 Charge Details (Include Ordinance or R.C.W. Number)

[ ] Additional persons on Report Continuation Sheet (People) Form No. Z-556   Juvenile Arrests - Block No. 109 MUST Be completed

VEHICLE

48 Stolen	49 Victim	50 Impound	54 License No.	55 Lic/State	56 Lic/Year	57 Lic/Type	58 Vin.
51 Recovery	52 Suspect	53 Hold					
59 Year	60 Make	61 Model	62 Body Style	63 Color	64 Peculiarities	65 Hold Requested by/For	
66 Ori. & Case No.	67 Registered Owner: Name		Address	City	State Zip	68 Home Phone	

69 Condition [ ] Drivable [ ] Not Drivable [ ] Stripped [ ] Wrecked	70 Inventory
70 Inventory (Continued)	71 Tow Co. & Signature

72 Enter	73 Date	74 Time	75 WACIC	76 LESA	77 Initial	78 Release Info	79 Date	80 Time	81 Release No.	82 Releasing Authority
83 Clear	84	85	86	87	88	89 Owner Notified	90	91	92 Operator's Name	

93 Signature & I.D. No. of Reporting Officer(s) A Morris (#301)	94 Approval	95 Distribution Excp.

REPORT PROCESSING (Records Personnel Only)	DISTRIBUTION: DATE _____ BY _____ INDEXED: DATE _____ BY _____	Microfilmed Initials _____	Filed Initials _____

C3:\C\P\J\POLICE.RPT

APPENDIX BB

NARRATIVE:

On December 22, Detective Daniel Stevens of the Nettletown Police Department gave us a copy of a tape recorded confession of juvenile Dailey (attached). The statement revealed that the juvenile made money selling bootleg tapes that he got from "a man named Gil." And further, that at one meeting there had been a man named "T-Cat" who had appeared to be in charge. The juvenile told Stevens that he put money and sales receipts for the tapes in Nettletown P.O. Box #609, which was consistent with other information we had. The juvenile also said he could recognize "T-Cat" if required.

TRANSCRIPT: James Dailey Interrogation

OF = Officer Files
OS = Officer Smith
DT = Detective Tevens
JD = James Dailey

OF: It's 1730 hours, December 10, Y-1, and this is Officer Files of the Nettletown

Police Department. I'm in interview room #3 at the main downtown police station

with suspect James Dailey. I've just turned on the tape recorder. James, please

state your name for the tape.

JD: James Dailey.

OF: And how old are you, James?

JD: 16.

OF: Now, from the time we arrested you at your uncle's ...

JD: That jerk. This is all his fault ...

OF: Why?

JD: He made me open my trunk with all the bootleg tapes in it. It was none of his

business.

OF: Uh huh. Anyway, James, from that time until now, no one from the police has

tried to talk about this case with you, have they?

JD: No ... I want to talk to my mom.

OF: I'm sure you'll get to, but first I need to talk to you.

JD: I want to see my mom.

OF: Later, James. First, I have to give you your <u>Miranda</u> warnings, OK?

JD: OK.

OF: Good. Here goes ... I'm reading off a printed card. You have the right to remain

silent. Anything you say can and will be used against you in a court of law. You

have the right to be represented by an attorney. If you cannot afford one, the

court will appoint one for you without expense. Do you understand these rights?

APPENDIX CC

JD: Sure. Just like on television.

OF: That's right. Now, having these rights in mind that I've just read you, are you ready to talk with me?

JD: No.

OF: Why not?

JD: I just don't want to. I want to see my mom.

OF: I'm sure if we talk about things a bit, we'll find a way to get your mom to see you.

JD: What do you want to talk about?

OF: How about where those tapes in your chest came from, for starters?

JD: I don't want to talk about that.

OF: Well, then, how about a place called "The Rancho"? Or mailbox #609?

JD: I don't want to talk about that either.

OF: What do you want to talk about then?

JD: Nothing. I want to see my mom.

OF: James, cooperating can make things a lot easier for you.

JD: What do you mean?

OF: I mean that if you have nothing more to say to me, I guess we'll just have to transport you to Juvenile Detention.

JD: Detention ...

OF: Yeah.

JD: I still don't want to talk to you. I want to see my mom.

OF: OK. No hard feelings ... Officer Smith, I think we've got a young man here who's going to spend the night in Juvie Detention.

[Next day]

OS: This is Officer Smith at Juvenile Detention. I've just turned on the tape. It's December 11, Y-1, at 1300 hours, and I'm with James Dailey who's just returned from a detention hearing at the juvenile court. James, state your name for the tape.

JD: James Dailey ... Do I really have to talk with you? Mom's waiting outside.

OS: This will just take a second, James. Just routine, OK?

JD: OK.

OS: Good. I hear you're free to go.

JD: Yeah, the judge said I could go home with mom as soon as I picked up my things here and signed some stuff.

OS: I thought you were living with your uncle.

JD: That slime-ball. I don't ever want to see him again. I was just with him for a few weeks because Mom kinda fell apart after Dad died. But she's OK now and we're moving back in the house together.

OS: Did you have a lawyer at the detention hearing?

JD: No. Just the Judge, D.A., me and Mom.

OS: No attorney.

JD: Well, they've appointed some public defender for me. Mom has the paper with her name. She'll be with me next time I go to court.

OS: Now, before you go, do you think maybe it would be better to talk about all this tape stuff with us. These guys you've been working for, they're the bad ones. They're the ones cheating honest musicians out of the money, making legitimate tapes more expensive for everyone, and using nice kids like you. But if you don't help us, they're the ones that will get away and you're going to take all the heat.

JD: I told that other guy last night ...

OS: Officer Files?

JD: Yeah, Officer Files. Anyway, I told him the same as I'm telling you. I don't want to talk. Now, my mom's waiting outside and I want to leave.

OS: Sure, James. No problem. But you see my side of it, don't you?

JD: I guess.

OS: Fine.

[Noise ... interruption]

OS: James, I have a note here that says that on your way out you're to see Detective

        Tevens.

JD: Who?

OS: Brad Tevens. I had the impression you knew him.

JD: Oh. Coach Tevens, sure. But I really want to get home.

OS: Of course. Oh, here he is.

DT: Hi, James.

JD: Hi, Coach Tevens.

OS: Well, why don't I leave you two teammates alone. Good luck, James.

JD: Yeah. Thanks.

DT: How are you, James?

JD: Oh, I don't know ... All right, I guess.

DT: I just saw your mom out in the lobby.

JD: Yeah, we're going home together.

DT: She really looks sad.

JD: Sure. She and Dad were real close. Since he died from cancer, she's really been

        lost. We all knew it was coming, but somehow when it did ...

DT: I can imagine how hard that must have been, but I don't think that's all. This

        trouble you're in seems to be really getting to her.

JD: How do you know?

DT: I can just tell. I have kids of my own, remember.

JD: Sure. How's Dave?

DT: Doing fine. You know, he's a sophomore at State. Really likes it.

JD: Great.

DT: Have you decided about college?

JD: No. I'm not much for school, and with this ...

DT: How long have I known you, James? 9 years?

JD: Sure.

DT: You were a little over 7 when I first coached you in the police baseball league, weren't you?

JD: Yeah … Coach Tevens, I shouldn't keep Mom. She's been outside awhile waiting for me. Maybe we can talk later.

DT: I know your mom won't mind. In fact, I know she'd want us to talk now.

JD: You sure?

DT: Absolutely.

JD: We had quite a team, didn't we? I mean, we won the league when I was in junior high.

DT: That was the best team I ever coached.

JD: Really?

DT: No question. And you. I'll never forget that catch you made in right field … Shades of Willie Mays.

JD: Oh, I wouldn't say it was that good. I just got lucky, that's …

DT: No way. You still playing ball?

JD: No. Not much.

DT: James, I just don't get how you go from a star ballplayer to selling those pirated tapes at school. You just have too much on the ball for that.

JD: I don't want to talk about it, Coach.

DT: Of course. I understand. I'm not asking you to talk about it. I'm just thinking out loud. It's just that I'm your old coach, and I worry about you.

JD: I know, Coach. But it will all turn out fine.

DT: That's the problem, James. That's what's tearing me apart. It's not going to turn out fine; not the way it's going.

JD: What do you mean? The judge let me go home with Mom.

DT: That's routine in juvenile cases before the merit hearing.

JD: I've never been in any trouble before, Coach. The judge said that when she said I could go home with Mom.

DT: This outweighs all those years of being good in spades. Trust me, James. This is my job. I've done it for over 20 years. I know. This is very, very serious.

JD: But it's only rock concert tapes. It's not crack. People have tapes they get in the store. What's the big deal?

DT: Theft. Conspiracy. Copyright violations. Possible federal stuff. This is the big time, James. You're only a little fish, but it looks like you're the only fish they have so far.

JD: What should I do, Coach?

DT: What do you want to do?

JD: I don't know. I'm scared. Am I in real bad trouble, Coach?

DT: Looks like it, James. Can I help?

JD: I don't know.

DT: Want to talk about it?

JD: I don't know.

DT: That's OK. You don't have to. It's just that if I can help ...

JD: Yeah. I'd like to talk to you.

DT: You're sure? I don't want to pressure you. I don't want you to do anything you don't want to ...

JD: Please. I need to talk to someone. Please help me.

DT: I'll do my best, James. But first, before we talk, I've got to give you these technical warnings.

JD: Officer Files already read me <u>Miranda</u>.

DT: Well, just to do it by the book and protect you and me, let's do it one more time. Is that OK with you?

JD: Sure ... Can someone tell Mom I'll be out in a while.

DT: Sure. [Whereupon Tevens calls the lobby desk to inform Ms. Dailey]

JD: Thanks.

DT: No problem. Where was I? ... Oh, yeah, <u>Miranda</u>. James. You have the right not to talk. If you do, I can take what you say and tell it to other police and the prosecutor and they might use it against you. You have a right to an attorney. If you can't afford one, one will be appointed for you.

JD: I already have an attorney.

DT: What?

JD: Yeah. Today. They gave me the name of a Public Defender who'll be my attorney the next time I go to court.

DT: Was this attorney with you in court today?

JD: No. She'll be there next time.

DT: Have you met with her yet?

JD: No. But you think we should call her?

DT: I have nothing to say to her. Anyway, I doubt we could reach her at this time.

JD: I guess you're right, Coach. Well, let me tell you ...

DT: Wait, James. First, do you understand the rights I've just told you?

JD: Yes.

DT: You sure?

JD: Yes.

DT: And mindful of those rights, do you still wish to talk to me?

JD: Yes.

DT: Have I or has anyone threatened you or made you any promises depending on whether you talk or don't talk?

JD: No.

DT: So your decision to talk to me is voluntary, of your own free will?

JD: Yes.

DT: Go on.

JD: Like it's this way ... you'll understand. This is between you and me, right?

DT: Go on, James.

JD: Mom needed money, the hospital bills and all ... Dad not being able to work. So, I made money.

DT: Uh huh.

JD: Selling pirated concert tapes is good money and I was saving almost all I made for her. Honest.

DT: I believe you, James. Tell me about the tape operation.

JD: What do you want to know?

DT: Let's begin with how you first got involved.

JD: It was ... it was over a year ago.

DT: When?

JD: Last June or July. I'm not certain exactly when.

DT: That's fine. Just do your best.

JD: Well, I was caddying. Trying to pick up a little extra money. Most of the time I was caddying for this guy, Mr. Ed Broil, over at the Northshore Club.

DT: Ed Broil?

JD: Yeah. Shot almost scratch. Real good tipper.

DT: Go on.

JD: One day we were talking, and he was saying what a good worker I was. You know, how a lot of kids my age weren't that dependable ... you'd make an appointment to meet them at a a certain tee-time and they'd cancel at the last moment so that it was hard to find another caddie or not even show up ... but that he knew that I'd never do anything like that and that he could count on me. And you know, he was right. I'd never do anything like that.

DT: I know you wouldn't James.

JD: So I thanked him and told him that I liked to work, that I wished I could work more. I think I might have also told him that I needed the money for my family. I'm not sure if I told him then. I know I told him at some point.

DT: What did he say when you told him that you liked to work?

JD: He said that he might just have some work for me.

DT: Did he say what?

JD: Not at that time. He said he'd have to talk to some people first and then get back to me. And then he asked if I was good at keeping secrets.

DT: What did you say?

JD: I asked him what he meant. And he said secrets, like if he told me something and told me not to tell anyone … not my mom or dad … dad was alive then … or anyone, friends, girlfriend, teachers, anyone … would I keep the secret, no matter what? Because that was real, real important to him and these other people he was going to be talking to.

DT: What did you think was going on?

JD: I didn't know. It was a little scary the way he said it, but it was also exciting. No grownup had ever asked me anything like that. And I can keep a secret, you know, so I told him that he could trust me.

DT: Uh huh. What next?

JD: Well, he didn't say anything the next two times I caddied for him, and I figured he forgot or things hadn't worked out or whatever. No big deal. I sure wasn't going to say anything.

DT: Did he ever say anything again?

JD: Sure. That's why you and I are talking Coach. The next time I caddied for him …

DT: How long was this from the first time he mentioned the job?

JD: A couple weeks.

DT: Go on.

JD: Anyway, the next time I caddied for him, after we were done, he asked if I had a few minutes to drop by his house before I went home. So I said yes, no big deal, and rode my bike over ... he wasn't that far from the course ...

DT: Where does he live?

JD: 90210 Melrose Place.

DT: Do you know his phone?

JD: No.

DT: Oh, yeah, what does Ed Broil look like?

JD: An old guy, maybe 45. Curly red hair and beard. Tall, over 6'. But kinda thin ... I don't know, you know, just an old dude ...

DT: Tell me what happened when you got over to his house?

JD: I don't know ... we just started talking about all kindsa stuff, you know, local sports teams, and high school babes, and music. He started to ask what music I liked and it was so rad, just about any group I mentioned, he had one of their concerts on tape. It was great.

DT: What then?

JD: He started to tell me what a rip-off the music industry is ... how everyone makes zillions and sells 10¢ worth of plastic for $10 or more and makes another gazillion bucks off of tours and that they would still be rich if they charged one-third as much, but they're greedy ...

DT: Do you know why he was telling you this?

JD: Sure. So I'd see that it was all right to pirate tapes and sell them.

DT: Did he tell you that?

JD: No. It just occurred to me later. He just asked me if I was still interested in getting more work, and I said I was. And he asked if I knew many kids at the high school, and I said I know everyone. I grew up with everyone; we've all been together since junior high and I've been with half of them since 1st grade. Also, I know a lot of kids at other local high schools, and I told him that, too.

DT: Uh huh. I guess you do know everyone.

JD: Sure. Well, he said that was perfect, and he'd talked to his friends and that they thought I might be right for the job. And I said "Great, when do I start?"

DT: What did he say?

JD: He laughed.

DT: Laughed?

JD: Yeah. He asked whether I wanted to know what the job is and what it paid before I accepted. Well, sure I wanted to know; what was it? And he said selling music, and I could make a lot of money. Then he went into that keeping a secret stuff again, and then he told me about the pirate tapes.

DT: What did you think?

JD: Then?

DT: Yes, then.

JD: No big deal. It wasn't like selling drugs or anything bad. A lot of the kids already had bootleg tapes we'd listen to. It didn't seem like a crime ... like I told you, making some money that would otherwise go to greedy zillionaires ... and maybe not even that, because you don't even know you're taking their money because a lot of kids wouldn't have bought the tapes at full price anyway.

DT: What happened then?

JD: We talked about how to approach people for sales ... you know, about telling them to be cool about talking about it or they'll kill the goose that's laying golden eggs. And then he explained how it would all work.

DT: How did it work?

JD: Well, every two weeks I'd get a sheet of our tape inventory.

DT: Where?

JD: In a post office box at the main post office. Box #609.

DT: What does this sheet look like?

JD: List of groups, concert dates, and the number of tapes for each in stock.

DT: Do you know if you were the only one selling?

JD: No. I don't think so. I got the impression from Mr. Broil that they had kids like me selling for them all over the state.

DT: What would you do then?

JD: Go around, take orders … And collect money. $4.00 a tape. I mean, that's like free. Sometimes I'd sell 300–400 tapes in two weeks. Kids would buy 4–5 for themselves, and gifts, and … I don't know, I think some may have resold them.

DT: Weren't you afraid that with so many people, someone would inform on you, or at least let something slip?

JD: Not really. As I said, it wasn't like I was selling drugs. Everyone thought this was cool, and they all understood it was important not to say anything too much about it.

DT: What would you do with the money?

JD: Put it with the order in an envelope and put it all in the post office box.

DT: Box #609?

JD: Yeah, #609.

DT: What would happen then?

JD: A few days later I'd get a carton with a copy of the order, my cut, and all the tapes.

DT: What was your cut?

JD: About $200 a shipment. $400 a month.

DT: Where would you pick up the carton?

JD: It was delivered to a different post office under the name of "Gro-green," a make-believe lawn supply company. But Mr. Broil had arranged it so the people at that post office thought I worked as a "Gofer" for the lawn supply company.

DT: Do you know where the cartons were shipped from?

JD: No.

DT: Were there any markings or return addresses on the cartons?

JD: A phony return address ... Uh, sometimes the word "Rancho" would be in magic marker on one of the cartons, but I never knew what that meant.

DT: How would you distribute all those tapes every two weeks without being obvious?

JD: It was real simple. All the students in the district have mail slots. You know, for announcements, messages from teachers, personal messages. I just tossed envelopes with the cassettes into the slots. No big deal ...

DT: Did you see Broil very often after you started working for him?

JD: Every once in a while if he golfed on the weekend and I caddied for him. Otherwise, not once school began ...

DT: Did you ever meet any of the people who were involved in this other than Broil?

JD: Only once.

DT: Tell me about it.

JD: I was walking to the store and Mr. Broil pulled up to the curb and called me over. There were these two other guys in the car. I'd never seen either one before.

DT: Can you describe them?

JD: Sorta. They were sitting down. But they were both Mr. Broil's age or older. One guy was big with blonde hair, the other was kinda fat with white hair and a white beard.

DT: Could you recognize these guys if you saw them again?

JD: Sure. I think so.

DT: So what happened when Broil pulled over?

JD: He asked me how I was doing, and I said fine. Then he said something like, "Gil, this is the kid I've been telling you about ... a natural businessman."

DT: What happened then?

JD: This Gil guy reached through the window and shook my hand and told me to keep up the good work. Then Gil said to Mr. Broil that he can tell that "T-Cat," that's what Gil called the other guy ... I think Mr. Broil may also have called him "Tom-Cat" at some point, but I'm not sure ...

DT: "T-Cat"?

JD: Yeah, "T-Cat" ... Anyway, this Gil guy said that he could tell that "T-Cat" was getting restless and wanted to move on.

DT: You think this "T-Cat" had anything to do with the bootleg tapes?

JD: Oh, definitely. Didn't say a word, just sat there ... but, you got the impression this guy was in charge.

DT: How?

JD: Oh. I don't know. You could just tell. I don't know, you just could ...

DT: Which of the two guys was T-Cat?

JD: The fat white-haired guy with the beard. Gil was the other guy.

DT: You look a bit tired, James. A lot's been happening and we've kept your mom waiting. Why don't we stop for now?

JD: Do you think you can help me, Coach?

DT: I'll try, but your continued cooperation will be real important ... You understand what I'm saying, don't you, James?

JD: Yes, sir.

DT: Good. Now go home with your mom and we'll talk later. Be sure and give her my best.

JD: Thank you, Coach.

DT: It's all right. I'm happy to do it.

IN THE SUPERIOR COURT OF THE STATE OF CASCADIA

COUNTY OF NETTLE

STATE OF CASCADIA,

              Plaintiff,

              v.

THOMAS L. KATSINSKI et al,

              Defendants.

)
)
)
)
)
)
)
)
)

NO. Y-1-9-01621-2

DECLARATION OF LIZ DORSETT
RE: Certification of Tape Transcription

I, LIZ DORSETT, say:

1. I am the Administrative Assistant for the Tape Fraud Task Force.

2. I am at least eighteen years of age and competent to transcribe tape # 848 dated 12/10/Y-1 and 12/11/Y-1.

3. I am not a party to this cause.

4. On May 28, Y-0, I listened to the tape more than five times and at various speeds.

I certify under penalty of perjury under the laws of the State of Cascadia that the foregoing is true and correct.

Date: June 1, Y-0

Place: Nettletown, Cascadia

                                 Liz Dorsett
                               LIZ DORSETT

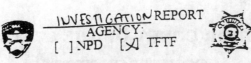

INVESTIGATION REPORT
AGENCY: [ ] NPD [X] TFTF
OTHER: _____

Page 1 of 2

1 Public Disclosure Act	OTHER:	

2 Arrest	3 Vehicle	4 Juvenile	8 Report Name/Offense
5 Property	6 Medical	7 Domestic Viol	TAPE FRAUD INVESTIGATION

9 Type of Premise (For vehicles, state where parked.)	10 Entry Point	11 Method

12 Weapon /Tool/Force Used	13 Date Reported 1.26.Y-0	14 Time Reported	15 Date Occurrence	16 Time Occurrence	17 Day of Week

18 Location of: Incident [ ] Address [ ]		19 Census	20 Dist.

PERSONS/BUSINESS INVOLVED

CODE C (Person Reporting Complaint) V (Victim) W (Witness) P (Parent) VB (Victim Business) O (Other)

21 Code	22 NAME: Last	First	Middle (Maiden)	23 Race/Sex	24 Date of Birth	25 Home Phone
26 DPA	27 ADDRESS: Street	City	State	Zip	28 Place of Employment/School	29 Business Phone

(repeated blank person rows 21–29)

[ ] Additional persons on Report Continuation Sheet (People) Form No. Z-556

PERSON NUMBER 1
CODE: A (Arrest) S (Suspect) SV (Suspect Verified) R (Runaway) M (Missing Person) I (Institutional Impact)

30 Code	31 NAME: Last	First	Middle (Maiden)	32 Home Phone	33 Business Phone
S	KATSINSKI	THOMAS	L.		

34 ADDRESS: Street	City	State	Zip	35 Occupation	36 Place of Employment/School	37 Relation to Victim
2023 CHERRY AVE.	Nettletown		00071	INSURANCE SALESMAN	REGIONAL INSURANCE	

38 Date of Birth	39 Race	40 Sex	41 Height	42 Weight/Build	43 Hair	44 Eyes	45 Clothing, Scars, marks, Tattoos, Peculiarities, A.K.A.
6.16.Y-44	C	M	5'9"	180 lbs	White	hzl.	beard/"T-C", "T-Cat", "Tom-Cat"

46 [ ] Booked [ ] Cited Number	47 Charge Details (Include Ordinance or R.C.W. Number)

PERSON NUMBER 2
(blank rows 30–47)

[ ] Additional persons on Report Continuation Sheet (People) Form No. Z-556   Juvenile Arrests - Block No. 109 MUST Be completed

VEHICLE

48 Stolen	49 Victim	50 Impound	54 License No.	55 Lic/State	56 Lic/Year	57 Lic/Type	58 Vin.
51 Recovery	52 Suspect	53 Hold					

59 Year	60 Make	61 Model	62 Body Style	63 Color	64 Peculiarities	65 Hold Requested by/For

66 Ori. & Case No.	67 Registered Owner: Name	Address	City	State	Zip	68 Home Phone

69 Condition [ ] Drivable [ ] Not Drivable [ ] Stripped [ ] Wrecked	70 Inventory

70 Inventory (Continued)   71 Tow Co. & Signature

72 Enter	73 Date	74 Time	75 WACIC	76 LESA	77 Initial	78 Release Info	79 Date	80 Time	81 Release No.	82 Releasing Authority
83 Clear	84	85	86	87	88	89 Owner Notified	90	91	92 Operator's Name	

93 Signature & I.D. No. of Reporting Officer(s) A. Morris (#301)	94 Approval	95 Distribution Excp.

REPORT PROCESSING (Records Personnel Only) DISTRIBUTION: DATE ___ BY ___ INDEXED: DATE ___ BY ___ Microfilmed Initials ___ Filed Initials ___

C3:\C\PU\POLICE.RPT

APPENDIX DD

NARRATIVE:

Following the search of the "Rancho," James Dailey was shown the photograph found in the search of Ralph Freely's cabin, and identified one of the men in the photo (the man with the "T.C." on his shirt) as "T-Cat." This photo was then placed on the police bulletin board. Patrolman Wayne Seltzer saw the photo and thought "T-Cat" looked like a man who had been booked after a mass arrest of demonstrators protesting Nettletown Ordinance #6. The arrests had subsequently been declared to be illegal by the court, but the mug shots were still on file. A search located the mug shot which matched "T-Cat." That, in turn, led to name and address of T.C., aka T-Cat, aka Tom-Cat, as Thomas Everet Katsinski, 2023 Cherry Avenue, Nettletown.

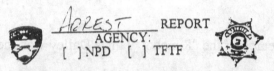

<u>ARREST</u> REPORT
AGENCY:
[ ] NPD   [ ] TFTF

Page 1 of 3

1	Public Disclosure Act	OTHER: _____	

2 Arrest	3 Vehicle	4 Juvenile	8 Report Name/Offense
5 Property	6 Medical	7 Domestic Viol	TAPE FRAUD

9 Type of Premise (For vehicles, state where parked.)	10 Entry Point	11 Method

12 Weapon /Tool/Force Used	13 Date Reported 1-29-Y-C	14 Time Reported 2100	15 Date Occurrence	16 Time Occurrence	17 Day of Week

18 Location of: Incident Address	[] TRAILER HOME	19 Census	20 Dist.

PERSONS/BUSINESS INVOLVED

CODE	C (Person Reporting Complaint)	V (Victim)	W (Witness)	P (Parent)	VB (Victim Business)	O (Other)
21 Code	22 NAME: Last / First / Middle (Maiden)				23 Race/Sex	24 Date of Birth	25 Home Phone
26 DPA	27 ADDRESS: Street / City / State / Zip				28 Place of Employment/School	29 Business Phone
21 Code	22 NAME: Last / First / Middle (Maiden)				23 Race/Sex	24 Date of Birth	25 Home Phone
26 DPA	27 ADDRESS: Street / City / State / Zip				28 Place of Employment/School	29 Business Phone
21 Code	22 NAME: Last / First / Middle (Maiden)				23 Race/Sex	24 Date of Birth	25 Home Phone
26 DPA	27 ADDRESS: Street / City / State / Zip				28 Place of Employment/School	29 Business Phone

[ ] Additional persons on Report Continuation Sheet (People) Form No. Z-556

PERSON NUMBER 1

CODE: A (Arrest) S (Suspect) SV (Suspect Verified) R (Runaway) M (Missing Person) I (Institutional Impact)

30 Code A	31 NAME: Last / First / Middle (Maiden)	32 Home Phone	33 Business Phone
34 ADDRESS: Street / City / State / Zip	35 Occupation	36 Place of Employment/School	37 Relation to Victim
38 Date of Birth	39 Race	40 Sex	41 Height	42 Weight/Build	43 Hair	44 Eyes	45 Clothing, Scars, marks, Tattoos, Peculiarities, A.K.A.
46 Number [X] Booked [ ] Cited	47 Charge Details (Include Ordinance or R.C.W. Number)

PERSON NUMBER 2

30 Code A	31 NAME: Last KATSINSKY / First THOMAS / Middle L.	32 Home Phone	33 Business Phone
34 ADDRESS: Street 2C23 CHERRY AVE. / City NETTLETOWN / State / Zip CC071	35 Occupation INSURANCE SALESMAN	36 Place of Employment/School REGIONAL INSURANCE	37 Relation to Victim
38 Date of Birth 6-16-Y-44	39 Race C	40 Sex M	41 Height 5'9"	42 Weight/Build 185 lbs	43 Hair WHT	44 Eyes HZL	45 BEARD/T.C.; T-CAT; TOM CAT
46 Number [X] Booked [ ] Cited	47 Charge Details 9.777 (CONSPIRACY) 15, C06(d) (PESSESS. OF BOOTLEG TAPES)

[ ] Additional persons on Report Continuation Sheet (People) Form No. Z-556   Juvenile Arrests - Block No. 109 MUST Be completed

VEHICLE

48 Stolen	49 Victim	50 Impound	54 License No.	55 Lic/State	56 Lic/Year	57 Lic/Type	58 Vin.
51 Recovery	52 Suspect	53 Hold					
59 Year	60 Make	61 Model	62 Body Style	63 Color	64 Peculiarities	65 Hold Requested by/For	
66 Ori. & Case No.	67 Registered Owner: Name	Address	City	State	Zip	68 Home Phone

69 Condition [ ] Drivable [ ] Stripped [ ] Not Drivable [ ] Wrecked	70 Inventory
70 Inventory (Continued)	71 Tow Co. & Signature

72 Enter	73 Date	74 Time	75 WACIC	76 LESA	77 Initial	78 Release Info	79 Date	80 Time	81 Release No.	82 Releasing Authority
83 Clear	84	85	86	87	88	89 Owner Notified	90	91	92 Operator's Name	

93 Signature & I.D. No. of Reporting Officer(s) #117. D. South #39	94 Approval	95 Distribution Excp.

REPORT PROCESSING (Records Personnel Only)	DISTRIBUTION: DATE _____ BY _____ INDEXED: DATE _____ BY _____	Microfilmed Initials _____	Filed Initials _____

C3:\C\P\\POLICE.RPT

APPENDIX EE

NARRATIVE:

At 2100 hours, RO and Officer Jay Johnson arrived at 2023 Cherry Avenue, Nettletown, to arrest Thomas Katsinski, a.k.a. T.C., a.k.a. T-Cat, a.k.a. Tom Cat. When we arrived at the Cherry Avenue address, the principal structure on the land appeared to be under renovation, and no persons appeared to be currently occupying this structure. Some 100 feet south of the framed house was a silver Air-Glide house trailer, approximately 20 feet long, on concrete blocks. There were curtains on the windows and a hose and electrical wires connecting the trailer to the house next door at 2025 Cherry Avenue.

Officer Johnson knocked on the door of the trailer, and a man who matched the picture we had seen of Thomas Katsinski answered the door.

We identified ourselves as police officers and asked if he was Thomas Katsinski. He indicated he was and took a few steps back as if inviting us in. We entered and I told the suspect he was under arrest. Officer Johnson handcuffed the suspect while I read him his rights as per Miranda v. Arizona. The suspect offered no resistance.

While Officer Johnson stayed with the suspect, I looked into the corner of the one-room trailer and saw a stack of cardboard boxes marked "Rancho" sitting in the far northwest corner of the trailer. I approached the boxes and saw the top carton was open. I looked in and saw that it was filled with cassette tape recordings. I thereupon seized all of the cartons and put them in the trunk of our patrol vehicle.

Suspect Katsinski was booked into Nettletown City Jail and the boxes of tapes were booked as evidence with the property clerk.

PROPERTY REPORT

AGENCY   NPD ◯   TFTF ⊗   OTHER _____   DATE 1·29·4-0

TYPE OF CRIME
Tape fraud

☒ EVIDENCE   ◯ FOUND
◯ SAFEKEEPING   ◯ OWNER UNKNOWN

LABORATORY WORK REQUIRED YES _____

RELATED CASE NO.

CENSUS   DIST.

PROPERTY OBTAINED FROM: ADDRESS   PHONE

V I C T I M	LAST NAME	FIRST	MIDDLE	S U B J E C T	LAST NAME	FIRST	MIDDLE
					Katsinski Thomas		L
	STREET ADDRESS	CITY	PHONE		STREET ADDRESS	CITY	PHONE
					2023 Cherry Ave. Nettletown		

PROPERTY INVENTORY					PROPERTY ROOM USE ONLY	
ITEM NO.	PROPERTY DESCRIPTION	QTY	SERIAL NO.	WA/NOC	LOCATION	RECEIPT NO.
1	boxes (cardboard cartons marked "Rancho") of cassette tapes of concerts - approximately 4,000 tapes	4				

PROPERTY SUBMITTED BY: J. Johnson (#423) UNIT NO: _____ DATE: 1·29·4-0
ADDITIONAL DESCRIPTIONS OR COMMENTS:

IOP ROOM USE ONLY	PROPERTY RECEIVED: METHOD _____ BY: _____ DATE: _____
	PROPERTY INVENTORIED BY: _____ UNIT: _____ DATE: _____

C2\CJ\PRP-RPT.FRM

Office of the Nettletown County Prosecutor
For the State of Cascadia
Investigations Division
Courthouse, Room 531
Nettletown, Cascadia 00077

Office # (001) 788-1200   FAX # (001) 788-1221

On 02/17/Y-0, at approximately 1030 hours, Susan Johnson and I, investigators for the Nettletown District Attorney office, spoke with SHELLY BRACKEN, 2035 Cherry Ave., Nettletown, Mr. Katsinski's neighbor. The electrical connection and hose to the trailer home where Mr. Katsinski was arrested ran to the Bracken home. Ms. Bracken was not able to furnish any information. Ms. Bracken said that Mr. Katsinski always was pleasant and that she never noticed anything unusual about him or his friends. When asked about the electrical cord and hose from the trailer home to her house, Ms. Bracken indicated that the trailer home was hers and on her land and that she was just letting Katsinski stay there "for a few weeks" while he was working on his house. A 2'-high wire divider at the edge of Ms. Bracken's garden divides her property from Katsinski's. [See attached Diagram.] The trailer stands on her side of this divider. Ms. Bracken denied knowledge of any of the cartons marked "Rancho" which were found in the trailer home at the time of Katsinski's arrest. Because another neighbor, Gil Jardine, had used the mobile home for several out-of-town friends prior to Katsinski using it, she could not say whether or not the cartons were there when she first let Katsinski use the mobile home.

APPENDIX FF

NOT TO SCALE

2023 CHERRY AVE.
(Thomas Kalsinski)

House
Under
Renovation

2' High
Divider

GARDEN

GARDEN

TRAILER

hose/
wires

BRACKEN
HOME
(2025 CHERRY AVE.)

N

APPENDIX GG

Office of the Nettletown County Prosecutor
For the State of Cascadia
Investigations Division
Courthouse, Room 531
Nettletown, Cascadia 00077

(001) 788-1200   (001) 788-1221 FAX

Spoke with Phil Reese on 2/24/Y-0 at 1045 hours. Reese had been in jail on drug charges at the same time Katsinski was in jail. On 2/12/Y-0, after Katsinski got out on bail, Reese had asked to meet with State Attorney General's Task Force on "bootleg tapes." Reese had indicated that he "could help" and was told that if that was so, maybe the Task Force could give him some help too.

Reese now reports that on 2/23/Y-0 when he got out on bail, he located Katsinski in an apartment at 2000 hours, and after a few beers, Katsinski told him "everything" about the bootleg tape operation at "The Rancho." Reese is willing to give details and testify against Katsinski if something can be done about the drug charges he is facing.

APPENDIX HH

NETTLE COUNTY SUPERIOR COURT
Courthouse

RE: STATE OF CASCADIA   Nettletown, Cascadia 00077

VS.

KEVIN M. LUMUS

Cause No. Y-1-9-0162-2
Violation Date: (6/Y-2 to 11/27/Y-1)

Violation: Conspiracy
Possession of Unauthorized Duplicated Copyrighted
Material

SUMMONS/SUBPOENA/NOTICE OF CASE SETTING

IN THE NAME OF THE STATE OF CASCADIA, YOU ARE HEREBY SUMMONED AND REQUIRED TO APPEAR ON THE DATE, TIME AND LOCATION STATED BELOW.

TIME: 9:00 a.m.

DATE: August 7, Y-0

COURTROOM: 603   JUDGE: Rolph
  ✓   COURT APPEARANCE IS MANDATORY.
_____ COURT APPEARANCE IS MANDATORY UNLESS $
_____ YOU MAY FORFEIT BAIL BY YOUR NON-APPEARANCE
cc: Pros. Atty:
       Officer:
       Defense Atty:
       Bondsman:
       Probation:

ARRAIGNMENT*
TRIAL
SENTENCING
HEARING
*See Reverse

CASH BAIL IS POSTED.

By: _____
             Deputy Clerk

APPENDIX II

*ARRAIGNMENT: IT IS YOUR FIRST APPEARANCE AND IS FOR THE PURPOSE OF ADVISING YOU OF YOUR RIGHTS IN COURT AND THE ENTRY OF YOUR PLEA TO THE CHARGE OR CHARGES FILED IN THIS COURT. NONE OF THE OTHER PARTIES CONCERNED WITH THE CASE WILL BE REQUIRED TO BE PRESENT AT THIS HEARING.

IF YOUR PLEA IS "NOT GUILTY" A TRIAL DATE WILL BE SET FOR A LATER DATE.

IF YOUR PLEA IS "GUILTY" YOUR CASE <u>MAY</u> BE DISPOSED OF AT THE TIME OF THIS APPEARANCE.

FORFEITABLE: THE OFFENSE YOU ARE CHARGED WITH IS FORFEITABLE AND DOES NOT REQUIRE YOUR APPEARANCE IN COURT ON CONDITION THAT BAIL HAS BEN POSTED PRIOR TO THE ARRAIGNMENT/PAYMENT DATE.

MANDATORY: YOUR ARE REQUIRED TO APPEAR IN COURT ON THE DATE INDICATED. THIS MANDATORY REQUIREMENT IS WAIVED ONLY ON THE CONDITIONS STATED ON THE FACE OF THIS NOTICE. FAILURE TO APPEAR AS DIRECTED MAY RESULT IN THE ISSUANCE OF A WARRANT FOR YOUR ARREST.

LICENSE SUSPENSION: FAILURE TO RESPOND, APPEAR FOR ANY HEARING, OR FAILURE TO PAY A MONETARY ASSESSMENT ON A TRAFFIC CITATION OR INFRACTION WILL RESULT IN THE SUSPENSION OF YOUR DRIVER'S LICENSE OR PRIVILEGE TO DRIVE UNTIL YOU HAVE PAID ALL PENALTIES REQUIRED BY LAW.

YOU HAVE THE RIGHT TO:

1. **BE REPRESENTED BY A LAWYER.** IF I CANNOT AFFORD A LAWYER, I HAVE THE RIGHT TO REQUEST A PUBLIC DEFENDER. IF I QUALIFY, A LAWYER WILL BE APPOINTED TO REPRESENT ME.

2. **A SPEEDY TRIAL** BY AN IMPARTIAL JUDGE OR JURY. IF I AM NOT IN JAIL ON THIS CHARGE I MUST BE BROUGHT TO TRIAL WITHIN 90 DAYS AFTER THE DATE OF ARRAIGNMENT. IF I AM BEING HELD IN JAIL ON THIS CHARGE, I MUST BE BROUGHT TO TRIAL WITHIN 60 DAYS AFTER THE DATE OF ARRAIGNMENT.

3. **A TRIAL BY A JURY** OF SIX (6) CITIZENS TO DETERMINE WHETHER I AM GUILTY OR NOT GUILTY, UNLESS I SPECIFICALLY GIVE UP THAT RIGHT.

4. **HEAR AND QUESTION ALL WITNESSES** WHO TESTIFY AGAINST ME AT TRIAL.

5. **CALL WITNESS** TO TESTIFY AT MY TRIAL AND THE RIGHT TO HAVE THE COURT ORDER THEM TO APPEAR.

6. **TESTIFY** AT MY TRIAL OR **TO REMAIN SILENT** BEFORE OR DURING MY TRIAL.

Kevin M. Lumus
200 Hampton St.
So. City, 00059

Nettle County Superior Court
Courthouse
Nettletown, Cascadia 00077

No. 16635

WARRANT OF ARREST

In the Superior Court
    The City of Nettletown

NETTLE COUNTY, STATE OF CASCADIA

        Plaintiff

      vs.

Name   Kevin M. Lumus
Address 200 Hampton St.
        So. City, 00059

        Defendant
        ss

STATE OF CASCADIA
COUNTY OF NETTLE
    The State of Cascadia to all Peace Officers,
Greetings:
    A Complaint/information under oath or certification
has been filed in this court, charging the defendant
with the crimes hereon described.
    Therefore, in the name of the State of Cascadia,
you are commanded to arrest the defendant and keep the
defendant in custody until the defendant is discharged
according to law, and make due return of this warrant with
your manner of service endorsed thereon. Cash or surety
bond to be approved by court. Service of this warrant by
telegraph or teletype is authorized.
Reason for Issuance:
☑ Failure to Appear for Arraignment
☐ Failure to Appear for hearing, Pretrial, Trial, Jury
☐ Failure to Comply with Conditions of Court Order
☐ Failure to Pay Fine
☐ **CASH BAIL ONLY**
No Personal Recognizance or Bail Bond

Bail		Court Case No.		Warrant Expiration Date
		Y-1-0162-2		8/7/Y+3

Originating Agency	Sex	Race	D.O.B	Hgt.	Wgt.	Eyes	Hair
Nettletown P.D.	M	C	11-1-Y-2	5'11"	137	bm	bm

Place of Employment	Social Security No.	Originating Agency Case #

Operator License No.	State	Expires	Citation No.	Violation Date

License Plate No.	State	Expires	Year	Make	Type	Color
BLA347	CAS		Y-3	Toyota	Celica	

Narrative	Ordinance
Wanted for conspiracy re bootleg tapes/possession of tapes	

Officer's Number	Complainant - Under Oath or Certification

Additional Identifying Data

I Hereby Certify That I Arrested the Named Defendant	Given Under My Hand This
On The _____ Day of _____ 19_____ Officer_____Agency_____ Service Fees_____ Service_____ Mileage_____ Total_____	7th Day of August Y-0 Judge/Commissioner _FRohr____

APPENDIX JJ

INCIDENT REPORT
AGENCY:
SOUTHCITY P.D.

1					
Public Disclosure Act		OTHER:			

2 Arrest	x	3 Vehicle		4 Juvenile		8 Report Name/Offense
5 Property		6 Medical		7 Domestic Viol		Out-of-County Bench Warrant

9 Type of Premise (For vehicles, state where parked.)	10 Entry Point	11 Method

12 Weapon/Tool/Force Used	13 Date Reported 8/5/Y+2	14 Time Reported 2115	15 Date Occurance 8/5/Y+2	16 Time Occurance 2115	17 Day of Week Thurs.

18 Location of: Incident [X] Address [ ]	Stopped for Taillight infraction on Prichcard Ave near intersection of Vermont Ln.	19 Census	20 Dist.

PERSONS/BUSINESS INVOLVED

CODE: C (Person Reporting Complaint) V (Victim) W (Witness) P (Parent) VB (Victim Business) O (Other)

21 Code	22 NAME: Last First Middle (Maiden)		23 Race/Sex	24 Date of Birth	25 Home Phone
26 DPA	27 ADDRESS: Street City State Zip		28 Place of Employment/School		29 Business Phone
21 Code	22 NAME: Last First Middle (Maiden)		23 Race/Sex	24 Date of Birth	25 Home Phone
26 DPA	27 ADDRESS: Street City State Zip		28 Place of Employment/School		29 Business Phone
21 Code	22 NAME: Last First Middle (Maiden)		23 Race/Sex	24 Date of Birth	25 Home Phone
26 DPA	27 ADDRESS: Street City State Zip		28 Place of Employment/School		29 Business Phone

[ ] Additional persons on Report Continuation Sheet (People) Form No. Z-556

PERSON NUMBER 1

CODE: A (Arrest) S (Suspect) SV (Suspect Verified) R (Runaway) M (Missing Person) I (Institutional Impact)

30 Code	31 NAME: Last LUMUS First KEVIN Middle (Maiden) M	32 Home Phone 835-9716	33 Business Phone SAME
34 ADDRESS: Street 200 Hampton St. City So. City State Zip 00095	35 Occupation Horse Trainer	36 Place of Employment/School Self-Employed	37 Relation to Victim

38 Date of Birth 11/1/Y-29	39 Race C	40 Sex M	41 Height 5'11"	42 Weight/Build 137 lbs	43 Hair brn	44 Eyes brn	45 Clothing, Scars, marks, Tattoos, Peculiarities, A.K.A.:

46 Number [X] Booked [X] Cited	47 Charge Details (Include Ordinance or R.C.W. Number) Taillight violation, So. City Muni Code 14-206C6) Nettle County Bench Warrant

PERSON NUMBER 2

CODE: A (Arrest) S (Suspect) SV (Suspect Verified) R (Runaway) M (Missing Person) I (Institutional Impact)

30 Code	31 NAME: Last First Middle (Maiden)	32 Home Phone	33 Business Phone
34 ADDRESS: Street City State Zip	35 Occupation	36 Place of Employment/School	37 Relation to Victim

38 Date of Birth	39 Race	40 Sex	41 Height	42 Weight/Build	43 Hair	44 Eyes	45 Clothing, Scars, marks, Tattoos, Peculiarities, A.K.A.:

46 Number [ ] Booked [ ] Cited	47 Charge Details (Include Ordinance or R.C.W. Number) Taken into custody on Bench Warrant #16635 (Nettle County)

[ ] Additional persons on Report Continuation Sheet (People) Form No. Z-556   **Juvenile Arrests - Block No. 109 MUST Be completed**

VEHICLE

48 Stolen	49 Victiim	50 Impound	54 License No.	55 Lic/State	56 Lic/Year	57 Lic/Type	58 Vin.
51 Recovery	52 Suspect	53 Hold	BLA 347				

59 Year Y-3	60 Make Toyota	61 Model Celica	62 Body Style	63 Color	64 Peculiarities	65 Hold Requested by/for

66 Ori. & Case No.	67 Registered Owner: Name Address	City	State	Zip	68 Home Phone

69 Condition [ ] Drivable [ ] Stripped [ ] Not Drivable [ ] Wrecked	70 Inventory

70 Inventory (Continued)	71 Tow Co. 7 Signature

72 Enter	73 Date	74 Time	75 WACIC	76 LESA	77 Initial	78 Release Info	79 Date	80 Time	81 Release No.	82 Releasing Authority
83 Clear	84	85	86	87	88	89 Owner Notified	90	91	92 Operator's Name	

93 Signature 7 I.D. No. Of Reporting Officer(s) L. Keever #633	94 Approval	95 Distribution Excp.

REPORT PROCESSING (Records Personnel Only)	DISTRIBUTION: DATE _____ BY _____ INDEXED: DATE _____ BY _____	Microfilmed Initials	Filed Initials

APPENDIX KK

NARRATIVE

At 2115 hours, August 5, Y+2, RO stopped suspect vehicle, a Y-3 Toyota Celica, license number BLA 347, for a taillight infraction. Driver identified himself as Kevin Lumus. A routine warrant check revealed a warrant from Nettle County. Suspect taken into custody and Nettle authorities informed.